The Whole Mishpocha

New and Selected Jewish Poems, 1998-2023

Philip Terman

Ben Yehuda Press
Teaneck, New Jersey

Published by Ben Yehuda Press
122 Ayers Court #1B
Teaneck, NJ 07666

http://www.BenYehudaPress.com

To subscribe to our monthly book club and support independent Jewish publishing, visit https://www.patreon.com/BenYehudaPress

Jewish Poetry Project #41 **http://jpoetry.us**

Ben Yehuda Press books may be purchased at a discount by synagogues, book clubs, and other institutions buying in bulk. For information, please email markets@BenYehudaPress.com

Cover illustration is "The Synagogue at Yarmolyntsi, Ukraine," a block print by Bill Farran reprinted by permission from his book *Lost Treasures: The Wooden Synagogues of Eastern Europe* (Independently published, 2023) www.billfarran.com or lostreasures@yahoo.com

ISBN13 978-1-963475-31-9 pb 978-1-963475-32-6 epub

Library of Congress Cataloging-in-Publication Data

Names: Terman, Philip, author.
Title: The whole Mishpocha : new and selected Jewish poems, 1998-2023 / Philip Terman.
Description: Teaneck, New Jersey : Ben Yehuda Press, 2024. | Series: The Jewish Poetry Project ; 41 | Summary: ""The Whole Mishpocho" is a collection of Jewish-themed poetry that explores the intricacies of Jewish life, identity, and heritage through a series of vivid, emotional, and thought-provoking poems. The poems delve into various aspects of the Jewish experience, blending personal reflections with broader cultural and historical themes"-- Provided by publisher.
Identifiers: LCCN 2024015775 (print) | LCCN 2024015776 (ebook) | ISBN 9781963475319 (paperback) | ISBN 9781963475326 (epub)
Subjects: LCGFT: Poetry.
Classification: LCC PS3570.E6763 W56 2024 (print) | LCC PS3570.E6763 (ebook) | DDC 811/.54--dc23/eng/20240408
LC record available at https://lccn.loc.gov/2024015775
LC ebook record available at https://lccn.loc.gov/2024015776

24 25 26 / 10 9 8 7 6 5 4 3 2 1 20240715

Also by Philip Terman:

My Blossoming Everything (Saddle Road Press, 2024)
I am a Jew: A Holocaust Family Memoir, with Susan Terman (Mammoth books, 2023)
Tango Under a Narrow Ceiling: The Selected Poems of Riad Saleh Hussein, co-translated with Saleh Razzouk (Bitter Oleander, 2021)
This Crazy Devotion (Broadstone Books, 2020)
Our Portion: New and Selected Poems (Autumn House Press, 2015)
The Torah Garden (Autumn House Press, 2011)
Rabbis of the Air (Autumn House Press, 2007)
Book of the Unbroken Days (Mammoth books, 2005)
The House of Sages (Mammoth books, 1998, 2005)

Chapbooks:

Like a Bird Entering a Window and Leaving Through Another Window
and *The Four Seasons* (with the painter James Stewart and bookbinder Susan Frakes, 2015)
Among the Scribes (Out and Back Press, 2013)
Greatest Hits (Kattywampus Press, 2005)
What Survives (Sow's Ear Press, 1993)

In beloved memory: Malka and Yussel

In beloved presence: Ganya, Mimi, Bella

Sever not thyself from the congregation.

Hillel, Pirkei Avot 2: 4

Contents

This Flickering World

The Service

Our Scriptures

Writing Jewish

The main sanctuary of Park Synagogue in Cleveland Heights, Ohio: its large room capped with a towering white-bricked dome, the walls a circle of windows. The rows of seats face the raised bimah where the ark houses the Torah, what is meant to bind us to biblical figures and to all Jews — past, present, and future. Today is a High Holiday, a Day of Awe — a day unlike the rest of the year, for on this day our names are scripted in the book of life and signed and sealed. Outside the leaves are on fire with autumn, the sky smoldering with dusk. This seeming opposition — the sacred text of the synagogue and the stunning beauty of the season — God's law vs. nature's law — provides for me an inviting poetic tension.

This holiness, the attempt to formalize a sense of being-in-the-presence-of-God, depends on one's sensibility. Approaching my bar mitzvah, the occasion was both serious and humorous, each mood represented by one of my parents. For my mother, it was solemn and spiritual, filled with beauty and transcendence; beside her I followed along with the Hebrew words of the prayers. For my father, it was an occasion to sleep. Once, on Yom Kippur, I pretended I had a stomach ache, giving him the opportunity to walk me home where we proceeded to watch the World Series. About both responses I've written poems: the sacred and the profane. In this sense, I, like many Jewish poets throughout history, "write Jewish." I draw heavily from the wealth of images, allusions, figures, and forms provided by a Jewish legacy which I have always understood, in agreement with Muriel Rukeyser, as an enormous gift.

Alternatively, many writers who are Jewish agree with Philip Roth, who considers himself a "writer first and a Jew second." And yet: Rodger Kamenetz, poet and author of *The Jew in the Lotus,* has said that his connection to his grandfather, and his grandfather's immigration experience, "is part of the reason I'm a Jewish poet and not a poet poet." If an American poet who is Jewish draws extensively from the pantheon of Jewish tradition, and does so with what Whitman calls "original energy," these poets are influenced as much by their Jewishness as by their English or American poetic traditions — and by "Jewishness" I mean the widest possible range. Few, for example, would claim that Kafka wasn't a "Jewish" writer; he himself, in his diaries, referred to his writings as a "new Talmud." This is not to suggest that the Jewish poet's work should consist only of this Jewish perspective — in fact, it's the intermingling of the Jewishness and references from other sources that expands a poem's reach.

About both responses I've written poems: the sacred and the profane. In my case, my Jewish education preceded my instruction in the international poets I was to read voraciously. My maternal grandmother, Gusty, who traveled at the age of 14 from a shtetl in the Ukraine, lived with us during my childhood years; to me, her presence represented the practicing Jew from Eastern Europe, much like the characters in the stories I encountered in Isaac Bashevis Singer, Sholem Aleichem, and Sholem Yankev Abramovitsh. And in our 1950's-style suburban bungalow, I could strongly identify with Philip Roth's Portnoy and Ginsberg's "America" and the whole Yiddishkeit mishmash with its humor and tragedies; its crazy superstitions and laws; its ambiguous relationship to God; the employment of the sacred in the everyday. We were conscious of being a people apart, living a double life. Growing up, we lived by another clock (it had Hebrew numbers) and another calendar (our new year in the fall); we didn't eat certain foods; we had different sets of dishes; we celebrated different holidays. For a child drawn to poetic language it was a veritable feast, a universe of sources one could celebrate and rebel against. My Jewish education provided me with an abundance of ancestral stories, imagery, tropes, allusions — a language I felt fortunate to write out of, that I could celebrate and — argue against, often in the same poem.

As I began writing and publishing my poems, I became interested in what inspired me on the deepest, most primal level: childhood, memory, ancestry, ritual. I combined my interest in Jewish themes and language with my attraction to the American free verse I was learning, primarily from the Whitman tradition. For example, Morris Rosenfeld and the other sweatshop poets who wrote in the early twentieth-century about their immigration experience reminded me of my grandmother, who worked at a dress factory, and even of my father, whose used car lot was a kind of latter day sweatshop. In his poem "Der Svet-Shop," Rosenfeld wrote: "Toiling without letup in that sunless den: /Nimble-fingered and (or so it seems) content,/ Sit with some thirty blighted women, blighted men, /With their spirits broken, and their bodies spent." I discovered a black and white photograph of around fifty women sitting before their Singer sewing machines in a sunless room: my grandmother was partially visible in the back.

Or the work of another Yiddish poet, Joseph Rolnick (from my ancestors' homeland, Belarus) who wrote a lovely and poignant poem, "Home from Praying," about the mysterious power of Jewish spirituality. It expressed the same feeling I had in the presence of the synagogue, the Ark, the sacred words. When he and his family return home from the synagogue on the Sabbath, he claims they "didn't recognize the barn and bridge, /the mill and house, /coming as we did from a different side/and at such an odd hour." A different side, an odd hour; yes—Judaism provides me with another dimension, another perspective.

The challenge, of course, for any poet writing from a particular tradition, is to not become trapped within that framework. It becomes important to both draw from and resist one's tradition, to find connections, echoes, associations, and tensions both within and outside of that tradition. Living in the country, on some acres, with an enormous garden and a Thoreau-like cabin overlooking a pond, I'm as inclined to read James Wright and Mary Oliver as I am the Psalms. I find creative energy in the tension between the Judaic focus on text and what the poet James Wright calls "the poetry of the present moment." That tension nourishes my writing, the space where both traditions meet—sometimes congenially, sometimes at odds, more often both at once...

What I continue to discover is that Judaism contains multitudes—it won't leave me alone, tempting me to draw from its infinite sources. Even as I attempt to write about our garden — we're clearing it out, pulling up tomato stakes, turning over the compost, gathering wood for a burn pile — I'm aware that it's early October, the season of the Jewish New Year: of the synagogue, with its large circular room crowned, like a huge yarmulke, with a towering white-bricked dome, the leaves on fire like pages from the Torah, the sky smoldering with dusk.

****

Among the Unspoken Names

We would be like the old Jews,
who knew nothing but devotion and gratitude,
every word was praise, praise, praise,

their bodies as the wind, their lives a poverty, their spirits
everything,
everything they spoke sang of creation,
their stomachs empty, lips parched, eyes hungry for the text—

the world was nowhere, even in summer,
even as the apples rounded and the quick birds flew
their quick flights from branch to branch,

even as sunlight spread itself, even dusk,
nothing could sway them outside those pages
to which they swayed.

We would be like the old sages—
for whom it was God this and God that,
nothing was as it was, everything was something else,
that blue jay, that grass, not blue only, not green only—

move closer, closer to the garden, how it floats under the
illuminated sky, softer, softer,
into that obscure place—

be nothing but an ear, they said.
Have you made arrangements? they asked,

about this hour, such as it is,
this hour of ecstasy and service, this document of mid-summer,
these days of drought and resurrection—

we would be like them,
we would turn into the book completely,

we would walk around the garden seven times
out of some obscure longing
we would ask our ancestors to explain,

we would be like the old interpreters,
whose words had wings,
we would climb the rungs of the ladder reaching up to the
bird's nest,

we would be as those scribes,
scribbling our sixteen hours a day, tonguing the sweetness of
the letters,
lost happily among the syllables—

if it weren't that we were stuck in the midst of all this beauty,
if it weren't for these children crouched in the apple tree,
faces flushed like apples, voices shrieking like blue jays—

we would know that the Madonna lilies are not Madonna lilies
only,
nor are the grapes their blood-purple, not their sweetness only...

Will our plantings flower as the dust?
Will our tomatoes suffer again their blight?

Or will the corn stalks be as scrolls lifted out of their dwellings,
bearing their fruit as plentiful as words?

We would, we think, be among the blessed,
the unspoken names,

we would be among the stories passed down,

if it weren't that we wanted to sing the whole thing,
the flesh of the earth, the consuming flames.

Small Boy, Unfathomable God

Silent Home Movie: The Bris

In sixty-five-year-old static,
on the screen torn at the edges,
my relatives again gather
around the living room table,
some familiar, some I reconstruct
out of dimly recalled stories.
They all hunch toward the center,
the men wearing yarmulkes,
the women shawled.
Two strangers stand aside
to reveal the eight-day infant,
myself, born of this house
and lying face up on the white
sheet, palms grasping for a mother's
absent hands. It is all black and white.
I squirm and cross my legs
as I watch the mohel wash
the thin blade in the glass
bowl of holy water, wipe it
against the towel my father holds
that soon will be stained
with blood. Fixing the knife
in the air, a few inches above
the chilled flesh, the mohel mouths
the words from the gold-plated
book: *This is my covenant,*
Which ye shall keep, between me
and thee, and thy seed after thee,
the blade slowly caressing
the private part of the shadowed
body, and in the blur
of spliced film, he slices
around the penis, the foreskin
thin as an insect's wing. Now,
everybody shakes hands—l'chaims,
mazel tovs without sound—

as I feel once more my heart
beating behind its outward flesh.

Donning Tefillin

Years it's been since I retrieved
the long white-fringed tallis
and the black thick straps

out of the blue velvet pouch,
a Star of David sewn into its side,
secured with a zipper, that my mother

safeguarded in a special drawer
beside her mother's two brass candleholders
and hand-knit shawl.

Rev Lev, our synagogue sage,
the Rebbe of our restlessness,
short and paunchy, hunched over,

a little like a schlemiel, voice off-key
as he taught us our Torah portions
in the small chapel beneath the main

sanctuary, instructed us one by one
to recite those passages of the story
that corresponded with our birth.

My arm would tense and turn
slightly purple as the Rev softly
guided my hand, his thick fingers

manipulating mine as we strapped
and then unstrapped the binds
seven times until it revealed

the flushed impressions of the spirals
along the length of my bare arm,
my skin slightly itching the way

it did, once, when the plaster cast
clasped around the broken bone, my arm
goose-pimpled, tiny hairs bristling,

my flesh burning to become a man.

The Everlasting Light

While in the other room the adults kvetched
about business and government and the history
of their complaints, our grandmother would call us
to the cupboard and pass around our Hanukkah gelt,
new silver dollars she'd kept hidden behind
her tin box of prayer books. She'd place the coins
in our hands with a blessing for the faith
in the everlasting light and then play us a game
of casino, her cotton dress splotched with flour
and sugar, her arms firm from carrying dishes
and setting the table, the labor of holiday.
And then we'd eat her famous latkes,
with apple sauce and sour cream, which all day
she'd prepare, grating and shaping the potatoes
stored, like her, in the cellar. She had her own sink
and stove and humidifier which could not keep out
the mildew. No windows and her hearing so bad
we'd have to blink the basement light on
and off from a switch upstairs to get her attention.
In her cabinet of dishes one side was meat,
one side was dairy, each piece of silverware
in its appropriate drawer because she'd cook only
according to the letter of the law using ingredients
that were blessed by someone she trusted to be wise.
After the meal, we'd gather and sing around the menorah
she'd place near the windows so the flames
could repeat themselves against the darkness.

At the Wailing Wall

And that last night, after everyone
in the hotel fell asleep, my mother
led me down the rough stones,
whitened by stars so close

we could touch them, to the square
in front of the Old Temple. She wrote
something on a scrap of paper,
placed it in a fissure with thousands

of others, forced it in tight
and hoped it stayed. *My message*
to God, she whispered. *You write one, too.*
The cracks were crammed

with petitions folded and packed in,
sealing the stones with pleadings
in that puzzle of boulders caulked
with tears and words and breath

whispered into the crevices.
We'd passed through the checkpoints,
our bags searched, our bodies
scanned and measured and judged

for that fragment, that chamber
of the original heart, that constellation
of oddly shaped stars fixed
in our shared sky, that calendar

that holds all our next years.
A flock of black-robed figures
requested us to follow them
down the stone steps into

a sanctuary beneath the wall,
thrusting shadows of books, pulsing
birds, into our quivering palms,
their eyes penetrating our flesh,

an obscure longing for us to take up
their responsive chanting, in that place
my mother's tongue spoke of all her life,
in that language she blessed me in.

Shalom Is My Middle Name

What my mother left me—
the word we should mean
when we say every other word,

the word we want to be more
than a word, the word I carry
tucked between other words,

from my birth to my death,
the word embarrassed
by its public display, preferring

its privacy, perhaps lifting
its first letter then retreating
back into the silence. But

there it is, stamped on my passport,
risking itself each time
it passes through security,

each time it wants to haul
its baggage from one country
to the next. Why, after all

these journeys, does it suddenly
step outside and assert itself,
aware as it is of the separations?

Why—
this hello, this goodbye,
this peace, this salám?

But in the Other World

for Jeff Goodman

He was my age but in the other world.
Twenty years he's been gone,
the same number than he had here
and so his time has been evenly divided,

balanced, the way he slowly stepped,
still wearing his yarmulke, along
the edge of the main sanctuary, over
the creek fifteen feet below.

We watched from a window:
halfway, he paused and stared down
into the water, like a rabbi
into a book, and chanted softly.

Our teacher yelled at us to back to our aleph-bet—
let him make his own self crazy!
And we turned to our exercises,
following the shapes of lines and dots,

connecting them up into a prayer
without wondering at the vocabulary
so that when we joined in the service
our voices would add to the praise.

His was always a little off-key,
his tone rising and falling, now monotone,
now imitation opera. He was silent
when the teacher isolated him in the corner.

He did what we wouldn't—
throw erasers at the loudspeaker,
gaze at the *Playboy* he'd cover up with his prayer book—
so when it came out he ate

the cyanide from the chemistry lab,
we knew was his way of getting attention.
His brother heard him say: *I'll see what happens.*
He's my age but in the other world,

where I can't help but think of him
now, how the years have gone,
and how the other side of my darkness
chants holy words to keep me balanced.

The Schvitz

If the Torah is our lives,
our portion was sung in that sanctuary
of a steam house by a minyan of ten

thirteen-year-old boys and a counselor,
a secular rabbi who knew the streets
like an emissary from the world

where our lives are already sealed.
He led us past the sign that still reads:
Members Only, listed in the phone book

as *The Russian Bath and Tea Room,*
but known to the initiates as *sweat*
in Yiddish, on 116th and Luke, our parents'

old neighborhood when all the world
was kosher and on Sabbath mornings
they walked in tennis shoes under

laundry drying above the street,
past houses of uneven boards
and sunken roofs, the fish market,

the famous Zeiger's Delicatessen,
before it changed, all except this small
brownstone, with a *mezuzah* on the door.

In the locker room I imitated his motions
as he took off his suit coat, muscles bulging
behind white shirt and tie, his pants,

the undershirt, the underwear, and I was afraid
to go on, to show myself in front of strangers.
Come on, he said, *here we're all the same, underneath.*

Cots with clean sheets lined
the central room. He instructed: *after*
we sweat, we rest. Adjacent, the dining area:

kosher pickles and hot peppers in bowls
under a photograph of the Wailing Wall:
after we rest, we eat. Steaks with garlic

broiled in the stove: *Then we go sweat some more.*
We were with history.
But all we knew was that we were naked

among men who were reading newspapers
or talking about how it was all changing
and the law was in our own hands.

Our counselor led us into the steam room
where old men sat on towels beside buckets
of cold water they'd pour over their heads

and fill up again. We began at the lower bench,
facing the hole in the wall where the sandstones
glowed like burning bushes, then moved up,

rising with the heat, daring the others to lie
full length at the top, long as they could stand it,
longer, until the room was so full of gray mist

we became outlines of figures floating
in a secluded heaven, simmering out
all of our small tensions, and still he'd say:

Throw in more water. It's not hot enough—
our heads down, my hands, like his, gripping
splintered wood against the oncoming rush.

Abraham's Breaking of the Idols

Abraham's breaking of the idols is one of my earliest stories,
and I imagined not the act of destruction, but the way
he climbed up on the roof all by himself and looked up at the
  sky
and imagined how it was all one thing—the stars, his thoughts,
even the pieces of the stone sculptures he smashed, even
his anger at his father for sculpting them, the way I was angry
at my father for how he'd sip his coffee and lean against
the sink before driving off to the work he hated so that I could
one day grow up and imagine Abraham inventing a religion
that included a father's obligations for his son. Now
it's the Sabbath, another result of that imagining,
and my own child is sifting sand from sand on a summer
  morning
so indescribably beautiful you can't help but grieve.
The shadowed wings of a turkey buzzard ascend the oaks and
  maples.
I heard that tale about Abraham in Sunday school.
I don't remember the weather—spring or fall—only that
Abraham was just my age, and now my daughter's age,
hiding from his punishment, but, nevertheless, listening.

When I Was Jesus Christus

In Saltzburg we studied German
and stayed in a pension where
the locals ordered schnitzels

and beer and the jukebox played
Mozart and Neil Young, across
the valley from the foothills

to the Alps and blocks away from
the Von Trapp mansion. I ran around
humming: *The hills are alive…*

This was 1978, and the cobbled streets
and *Mozart Platz* were haunted
by amputees, shadowed by the *Festung*.

I was young and tall and bearded
and Frau Steiner and all the locals
called me *Jesus Christus*. She liked me.

She chuckled at but admired my poor
attempts to order food *auf Deutsch*.
When Bradley, our graduate assistant,

was caught stealing from the common
refrigerator, the Frau came close
and asked: *Ist Bradley ein Jude?"*

Mozart stopped, the locals looked up,
as if I could confirm something
they all suspected. Lifting my full height,

I pointed to my chest: *Ich bin ein Jude!*
Frau Steiner nodded: *Ahhhh…ja, ja, ja…*
danke, danke, Jesus Christus.

Eloquence

". . . for I am slow of speech, and of a slow tongue."
—Moses to God

Born defective, roof of mouth
splintered, a cracked bowl,
pallet cleft like tabernacles.
My speech was impeded, my S's
slurred, my R's never rounded out,
and I knew to repeat myself like
a foreigner, as if my first was
my second language. Kids made
their usual fun: *Listen to the one with*
the bone in his mouth. In speech class,
I resisted reshaping the figures
my tongue made in the shelled spaces
of the cheeks, the air between teeth,
quivering upward like a needle
in its compass, into the deep gulf
of the North, where I exiled unsaid
syllables, at home in their deformed
privacy the way, I learned, the tongue
of Moses clung to its dome. Pharaoh
gave him a choice of gold or live coals.
No god, Moses reached for the coins,
but the angel descended to push and fold
his fingers over what was torn out of
the earth and on fire, charring the flesh
Moses quickly pressed to his lips, scorching
his tongue, a small bush burning.
His brother was his voice, his mouthpiece
before the people, but when he conversed
with the silence, as I write on this page,
he wandered off by himself and spoke alone.

My Bar Mitzvah Portion

—1 Samuel 20:18-:42

The story of Jonathan and David:
how they found favor
in each other's eyes,

and how there was a step of death
between them and King Saul—
I memorized the Hebrew words,

the dusty thirty-three vinyl
Rev Lev recorded for my edification.
Barely thirteen, I sang how they went out,

both of them, into a field,
where they made covenant,
and I revealed how each of them

loved so much the other
with his own soul that Jehovah
would be witness between them

forever. When they parted,
I insisted that they kissed,
those two men, and wept—

to make me a man.

Days of Awe

On Rosh Hashana

Like no other time of year,
we gather to remember
who we are and where we belong,
migrating the way certain birds
will return to the same place

the same time each year.
Our sanctuary was so full
they had chairs off to the side,
facing a wall, the cantor's liturgy
amplified, booming across

the domed House of God the way
we imagined God's voice
would have bellowed down
from the mountain or out of a bush.
We took our cues from others—

they rose and we knew the great Book
was taken out of the ark and lifted
onto the rabbi's shoulder's—they sat
and we knew it was returned
and the silk curtains closed delicately.

Ten years old, I looked into the thick
black book, wondering at the lines
and dots, and why they all read
from right to left. My mother
moved her lips and turned the pages and so did I,

thinking only of how I missed
the World Series, again. My father
had his book closed, head down.

I whispered to my mother, hand
on stomach: *I feel sick.*

My father offered to take me home.
We squeezed between worshipers out
into the still warm October air, the dark,
the large spaces the streets offered.
What we talked about I don't remember.

Only how clear with stars the night was.
And how big and tall was that man
made out of meat and potatoes,
and how the whole way home we strolled
side by side into the New Year.

First Sin

Enormous synagogue, Yom Kippur service.
Surrounded by a sea of congregants.

Our seats so far removed
from the bimah the rabbi
was only an amplified voice.

Needing to escape,
whispering to my mother: *I have
to go to the bathroom.*

Crawling past the worshippers,
the usher, through the door
and down the hall—

the drinking fountain—
throat parched, pushing
the silver button, bowing
to the flowing cold water.

And I sipped. And then I gulped.

I lifted my head, turned towards
the shadow of the usher's chastisement.

Small boy, unfathomable God.

All Vows

I was not ready to chant the Kol Nidre,
yet nevertheless I was called up
to stand before the open Ark

and find within myself the voice
that was required of me, the voice
hidden in the deep down, below

my errors, my words spoken
in haste, my actions taken
without thought, the hurts I caused.

The fast had begun.
The ark was open,
the Torah revealed,

the worshippers risen
in their white garments,
the rabbi nodding: *It's time,*

and, though I was not noble,
or virtuous, and though
my wrongs were a weight

I could barely hold, the way,
at the dawn of my adulthood—
almost another lifetime ago,

my muscles tightened to lift the Torah
and carry it around the shul,

pausing at each row of pews

for the congregants to touch
the scrolls with the fringes
of their tallit then their tallit to their lips—

something about the circumstances
of my life brought me to face
the sanctuary and the souls

who stood waiting
for me to confess release from our flaws,
and rejoice, with trembling.

Avodah

for Michal Gray-Schaffer

The rabbi prostrates herself
before the open Ark during
the holiest moment

on the holiest day, chanting
the prescribed aching pleas
so that each congregant

should live another year,
her fist beating her breast,
her body bowed low, kneeling,

begging to the spirit of the scrolls
to wash away our iniquities
and inscribe each of us into the book

because we turned away
from our hours
and gathered in this sanctuary.

Now she collapses facedown
on the carpet,
her body quivering beneath

the eternal light.
I'm one of her servants,
called up to assist in her prayer

of forgiveness, when she assumes
all of the congregation's sins
onto herself, as it is written.

Embracing one of the scrolls
as if it were a lover,
I shift its heavy weight

from shoulder to shoulder,
my arms straining,
knuckles whitening, hands

loosening with the fear
that these words of creation
and generation will slide

through my arms and spill
across the synagogue
and it will be impossible

for the worshippers
to put them together again.
I grasp them tighter,

as if carrying my own child,
listen hard as the rabbi beseeches
for our lives all the way

to the last note of the blessing.

The House Without a Clock

The house without a clock,
the flourishing scarves,
the swaying shadows,
the book cupped in the hands,
the pages on fire,
the choir of the blessed.
I was a candle of constancy,
a flame against September's spectacle.
I was a short word in the service,
awe in a child's body,
a small scroll lifted into the silence
we rose up towards.
I stood in the sacred perpetual, paused,
stared into our portion, and sang.

L'Dor va'dor

The Fates

Mrs. Sperling,
Mrs. Meadow,
my grandmother, Gusty—

dusk, porch, shadows,
robed in cotton dresses,
buttoned-up sweaters,

hair tied back in buns
under babushkas,
wire-rimmed spectacles

and heavy black shoes.
Twittering in Yiddish.
Even when young

they looked old. Each
had at least one deaf ear,
how they looked directly

at you when you spoke.
Hidden in their nest
perched in the Buckeye

that darkens its leaves
every evening.
Three widows from across

the waters. They've returned.
I want them to rest awhile
after their long lives of labor

before they spin and weave,
these birds of some exotic
species not recorded

on anyone's life-list,
relaxing their shoulders
as the shiny brown fruit plunks

into the grass. I place one
in each of their dough-crusted
hands, reciting Basho:

It is a common flower
the worldly think not worth
their note, chestnut

at the hermit's eaves.
I want them to kibbitz
about nothing we should

be concerned with
until the next millennium,
or the one after.

The Famous Ukranian-Jewish Woman Poet Termanovsky

If you found out your great-grandmother
was a poet, if there was one obscure book
you discovered one off-day at the bottom

of a dusty cardboard box, in the corner
basement room, covered up by pickle jars,
slid behind your father's war uniforms,

a volume slim as a small hand, the cover
a faded blue, layered and sealed with mold,
the pages tearing with a touch, the letters

in Yiddish, and there's her name: *Termanovsky*,
your name, before shortened by the authorities,
the way they'd slice off anything unpronounceable.

Termanovsky, the famous Ukranian-Jewish woman
poet, her daguerreotype on the title's facing page,
her face, the one you recognize from worn photos,

but younger, a beauty, no babushka—a frilled scarf
wrapped around the neck, her dark thick hair
flowing from beneath a tilted-to-one-side beret,

a few strands loose across her cheeks, dangling
from her lips a cigarette. You examine the strange
letters, lines, stanzas, wonder about

the pressure of her fingers pressing the pen
to the page, between the poverty and the pogrom,
the praying for a relative to sponsor her over,

the baking of the bread she had to peddle
in the marketplace, having to worry about who
would print and publish poems by a woman

named Termanovsky about being a girl
in the shtetl, the smell of herring and challah
rising, horses and wagons in the open air,

the mud streets, the learned huddled toward
the eastern wall, old men in black coats, how
it shamed her to have to sit on her side

of the synagogue—even if she had the space,
even if she had the time to save her moments
in words, the way she kept buttons in a box,

and was assured of the support to write them all down.

My Grandfather in Green

Chagall, you must have known my grandfather
who lived in the same province, perhaps
a few shtetls away, and who peddled fruit
and scrap with his one-eyed horse and so must
have shouted out his wares on the dirt road of Vitebsk,
your village, and you must have, turning aside
from the blank canvas looking out the window above
the town, listened to his hawking Yiddish and noticed
his pauper's cap and rabbinical rhythms, then turned
to your brushes and pallet and began, this time
with gusto, your *Jew in Green*. You invited him
to sit his weary overcoated slouched body down
on a couch of shadowed sacred texts, his face
lowering, as if in mourning, into his yellow beard,
his eyes distracted—such sadness you painted!—
He came, sat down, and at once fell asleep, you said,
exhausted as he must have been from hours
floating above the town, his enormous figure
lifted beyond the snow-covered roofs
and blue-tiled churches and empty streets,
leaning forward as if navigating the wind
with cane in hand and yellow sack slung
back over a shoulder—yes, that was him,
Yussel, my grandfather you painted—
Did you get his permission? The one, who,
in this thumbed photo, is dressed like a rabbi
with black cap and white garment shawled
the length of his body so he could, as it
was written, touch the blue fringes and remember
God and the commandments? Did you put him
on the canvas to get one more Jew out
of harm's way? Did you want my grandfather
to represent the Holy One the whole village awaited,
a symbol for the drunkard for whom everyone poured
a glass of wine, the hunchback slouching
throughout their dreams of poverty and miracles?

I want to know more about that green Jew,
  and the Jew who sniffs the snuff, who stares
  into an inward space, his eyes fixed above the text
laid open on the table, spread with yellow light.
  I'd like to think that figure was Yussel, too, inhaling God,
  his whole body sweetened by the habit—
because here it is mid-February, zero to the bone,
the workday world about to begin,
  the air turning gray, then grayer, then dark—so
  mostly, I want to lie down beside the reclining Jew at dusk,
patches of light splashed through the grass,
  the spruce trees, horse, pig, house, lilac sky beyond,
  his thin arms crossed over soft blue smock, hatless, musing
on love, of course, and beauty—Yussel, Yussel—
  Did he imagine you a dreaming poet, too?
  Did this insatiable artist paint you into the immortality you
  deserve?

The Dress Factory

And maybe that's why, after my grandfather
the junkman passed away, she contented herself
with my parents' basement: a small stove,

a refrigerator, an ironing board, an electric
heater, a sewing machine—a Singer,
foot-pedaled, like the ones in this photograph

where Jewish immigrant women of childbearing age
assembled after the storm-wind of 1905 ripped them
from the shtetl where the Bible was daily news.

And in their wooden synagogues and homes, sunken
around the marketplace, the streets winding tortuous
as a Talmudic argument, the hard years would give way

to redemption. But all they knew was massacre
and forced conversion, so they departed, hungry
to earn a living, America on their lips.

Here, in this enormous tenement of high temperatures
and bad lighting, gaslights hang from ceiling pipes,
blazing the black machines: workshop,

sweatshop, square room of concrete and brick,
the claustrophobic air absorbing their exile—
overcrowded and everywhere cloth, cloth, cloth,

spread out, shaped into garments, hung limply
on racks, seven dollars a week, in the dirt and dust,
fingers gathering and ruffling, basting and pleating,

embroidering, feet tapping in rhythm on iron grills, treadling
pedals, a seamstress dance, shoulders hunched over
into premature curvature of the spine, back-aching,

hair tied back in buns, hands spooling string,
a constant motion, joints aching their way to arthritis.
A million miles from birth, semi-skilled,

and there were always replacements.
And when would they look into a holy book?
Do they kibbitz about their peddler boyfriends

as they risk tuberculosis, the tailor's disease?
Do they fear the soup kitchens?
Some look toward the camera, others persist

at their needling, unaware that a hundred years later
one of their grandchildren will identify his own:
near the only window, wearing a schmatta

over a cotton dress. She will repair my clothes
from her supply of worn fabric or replace a button
from the tin box stored in her basement closet.

Ignoring the commotion, she will lean toward
her own steady center, lick and follow the thread
through the eye, the way she labored, dark

to dark, all her life, save for the Sabbath.

My Grandfather's Scale

A hinge creaking into another world,
the moment I lift my eyes toward
my grandfather's ancient scale
he'd measure the fruit with then peddle
the narrow red-brick streets of Cleveland's
Jewish section, its black numbers fainted
through scratched glass, the frayed rope
holding the container that weighed
the fruit that measured his hours:
It's a living, he' d say, and now it hangs
in the kitchen window, cradling the apples
we picked from our tree hours ago.
It's a living, he'd repeat, hauling the produce
in his horse and wagon and soon he was
in the junk business. He wore his hat,
like Whitman, inside and out. He ate
mustard from the jar. He just missed
the Titanic. When he was six,
in the Pale of Russia, where because
of his birth and belief he was exiled,
he was wrapped in a prayer shawl
and presented to the synagogue
to become intimate with
the Holy of Holies. All of his life
an acquaintance with the eternal
so when he went from one junkyard
to another he could in his mind chant
any of the 613 commandments and
perhaps the One whose name could
not be spoken but to whom he
could speak would be listening.
The scale is holding still and
balanced, the way he would cup me
in his stubby and scarred hands.
He died soon after. I never knew him
the way we mean the word so this

workaday object, this work of art,
with the fainted words: *tested*
and *sealed* and *Ohio* is all I have
of his outward life, his living
my inheritance.

L'Dor v'dor

Matza and Eggs

Sunday mornings my mother and I would walk up
the corner to Davis Bakery where the old Jewish women
behind the counter filled the room with kibbitz-song
and spinning around and around the perfect circles
of their famous creations; the egg, the onion, the raisin,
the plain, still warm and waiting to be opened and spread.
It was all pastry: the coconut bars, the Russian tea biscuits
with their layers of strawberry and walnuts, sugar and dough,
the loaves pregnant with rye, pumpernickel, even the challahs
they'd place on request into the ancient silver slicer,
its rusted blades rattling like my grandfather's junktruck along
the cobblestones of Hough Avenue. But we would only buy a box
of matzah, the bread of our affliction, to crumble and fry with egg, dip
in grape jam with our fingers, smooth the crumbs away with our tongues.

Again, These Blintzes

Month ago you rolled the thin pancakes around
the cottage cheese and froze them for this December
morning, as the sun glistens the ice-crusted branches
and snow weighs down the spruce needles. Now,
you heat them on the cookstove and I wake, the way
my grandfather woke, to the smell of dough frying in butter.
We smother them with sauce from the strawberries
we picked and sliced and mashed with sugar and stored
last summer or was it the summer before last? I'm confused:
how time slips—sour cream sticks in the hairs of my beard.
O is it my grandfather's tongue that savors each crumb?
Slender hours rolled like crepe around our preserved souls,
sweet fruit of recurrence, these Ukrainian delicacies—
each taste swallows me back to him, that peasant rabbi.

The Shema

If I sing a prayer I learned from my Ukranian Bubbe
to teach my Chinese daughter to sing before sleep,
has it traveled around the world? And
if that song is the same declaration
I chanted to my mother each night,
the same words congregations rise up
and recite before what they affirm to be
God's oneness, are we participating
in something beyond understanding?
How centuries of this agreement bring us
to this moment— the room dark except
for the pool of nightlight illuminating
her small ceramic tea set, her pink alarm clock,
the words sealing into her measured breath.

Teaching the Mourner's Kaddish to My Daughters

Forget the original Aramaic or Ezekiel's vision
that served as inspiration. I just hope for the Hebrew.
But they prefer the transliteration— which, no matter
the alphabet, translates into *magnification*. Thinking
of the rabbi building a fire in the woods and reciting
a prayer. And who was the rabbi and where were the woods
and how the fire was built were all forgotten. But not the prayer,
never the prayer—children, this is the one sad song
I do not wish you to sing, elegy of sorrow, gate of grief
I would forbid you to enter, these same syllables mourners
have pronounced for millennium and that I rise to chant,
according to their anniversary, for my father, my mother,
my brother, the rhythms you will enrich with each repetition.
Chant it again, sweethearts, from the beginning, more slowly.

My Mother Argues with Ecclesiastes

At the Wailing Wall, when she danced
with the dancers—that was her time,
that was her place—she ate and drank

and enjoyed all the good of her labor—
and now, her body struggling each breath
under the purple comforter,

her right hand holding the white sheet,
her mouth slightly open,
her pale cheeks sunken,

her pink gown open at the breasts,
her eyes, delicate as moth wings, closed—
this almost-death-mask,

these last living moments—is it true,
as it comes to pass, that all
is emptiness, these words, this effort? —

loving all, trusting few, always having
something in reserve: if she had one,
she needed two, she'd say,

if she had two, she needed three,
the way she wouldn't trust the banks,
a little of her fortune in each,

or her sons, a little of her wisdom
for each, not all for one, not the whole
in one heart, in case it breaks,

and you're left, she'd say, with nothing.
And here I am, a good son,
or trying to be, at her bedside,

reading to her through her Alzheimer's
and her stone-deafness and her dying,
from *Ecclesiastes,* who she interrupts

with her characteristic *chutzpah*:
No, you schlemiel! she shouts,
the day of death is not better than the day of birth!

Are you meshuggah?! she continues,
embarrassing me in front of this wise preacher:
The house of mourning is not greater

than the house of feasting!
Have you ever had children?
Have you ever had the blintzes at Corky and Lenny's?

Have you ever heard Jerry Vale's 'O Sole Mio'?
Have you ever drank four cups of wine on Passover?
Eat, drink and be merry—there we can agree,

yet with this breath that came to my bones
in her womb I continue to read to her:
Sorrow is better than laughter,

and I know she's ready to sue him,
she's asking for his name and number
in this, the beginning of her ending,

under the purple comforter.
One generation passeth away, I continue:
there is no remembrance of former things;

neither shall there be any remembrance
of things to come, and my mother rises
again to kvetch: *Is this man a putz?*

Is he blind? Is he not—pointing to me—
my afterlife? Her breath is slowing now,
the nurse applying delicately the morphine,

yet she continues: *Can't you see the bone*
of my bone? The flesh of my flesh?
And so will I in fact carry her

with me all the days of my life?
And what will she carry, empty of her body,
the air her sanctuary? Afternoons

we'd nap together, the shade drawn
against the sharp light, and we'd play the game
of who-falls-asleep-first, her assuring

breath, inhaling time, exhaling chance,
under the purple comforter,
arguing with Ecclesiastes, from beginning to end.

A Cast of Thousands

My dad's kid brother, Hy,
worked fourteen-hour days
at Cotton Club Soda Factory
through the Depression and the War,

dreaming of stardom. Eighteen,
wavy black hair, six foot six, dimples,
everyone's head would turn
when he'd stride like an undiscovered star
through the double doors

of Corky and Lenny's Delicatessen
where you would take a number
and order the smoked fish, the lox,
the spicy corned beef, the herring
in wine sauce and sour cream

from the old women in red *shmattes*
speckled with vanilla splotches,
faces patched with rouge and lipstick—
wishing all the customers a *mazel tov*
and filling the air with their *kibitz* songs—

You vant I should slice the challah?
What's the matter, here you think
it's not fresh?—In the clatter
and clutter from the meat counter
and the *kvetching* in the corner booth

where the alter kockers gathered
and kibitzed about the machers and the k'nockers.
My father had his own parable
about the man who was paid a ruble
per day to wait by the Eastern Wall

for the Messiah: "*How can you work*
for such low wages?" they asked the guy.
He replied: "Low wages, sure.
But at least the work is steady."
His brother, though, hitchhiked all the way

for a role in *The Ten Commandments.*
He played a slave,
then went into real estate. Each year
it appears around Passover, like Elijah,
and we'd watch close,

my father suddenly pointing to the set:
There he is!
No, wait, there he is!
No, no, I'm sure this time! It's him!
all of us straining for the familiar face.

He's still the one everybody asks about.
Some days, when it's dark early,
my father comes home from the used car lot,
kicks the snow off, tells us how none would start
and it seemed his blood would stop

and we should all be in California.

What We Own

For Bruce Terman (1952-2006)

I followed you down the switchback trail of the Grand Canyon
and we slept in a crevice, and we own that,

and we own those moments tossing the football in front of
4073 Wyncote Road until the streetlights snapped on,

and we own the smoke bomb the cops threw at us and a few
thousand others at the Jefferson Airplane concert, Akron,
Ohio, 1972,

and we own the whole country we passed through, all the
way to the ocean, where we checked into a hotel and you
discovered, lying atop Gideon's Bible,

a black film canister's worth of weed and half-a-pack of rolling
papers, and we smoked it, and it was good, unbelieving of
our luck,

which we own, and the lunar landscape surrounding our tent
in Big Bend, Texas, and the stars, so clear we could read by
them, and did,

and we own *The Godfather*—Part One—on the big screen of
that packed theater in Evanston, Illinois, and we own that
fear

when we were lost in the Tennessee woods, into the dark, and
you followed some analytical instinct until we found—lo and
behold—a road,

and Bob Dylan, who was ours, and Joan Baez, who was also
ours, singing "The Times They Are A-Changing" in the War
Memorial,

and watching the Indians—miracles of miracles—beat the
New York Yankees at Yankee Stadium during the 1995
heatwave—that, too, that victory, was ours,

and I remember how quiet you sometimes were, and I asked
about it, and you said it's a feeling you get, you don't know
how to talk about it, and I'd like to think

we own that feeling—how we bested the myths. We didn't
become murderer and victim. We didn't cheat on the other's
birthright.

Oh, my brother of the other world, my brother who perhaps
will greet me when I arrive at that place prepared for by our
father,

who is now joined by his own flesh and blood, which is not
blood, which is not flesh, but bones and perhaps spirit,

which we believe in, like the moon, or the unpredictable
Cleveland weather, or the way the snow descends on the
fallen leaves,

or how the sun glazes them now, for their moment, stirred in
the slight wind, the same wind that blew the Jerusalem dust
in our faces, which we own.

God's Speech

My parents were most in love
when they spoke the Yiddish
they remembered, sounding like

exotic birds or a soundtrack
to a film they starred in, more romantic
without the subtitles,

which would have revealed
their workaday conversation:

an ander mshuge tog—

but it was the other world,
it was God's speech, what
they didn't want to pass on,

that language that killed
their cousins, that language
their parents suffered
not to speak. But

they sometimes *fargesn*
and slipped into the *oy gevalts*
and the *sheyn punims*
of their childhoods, which,

against their best intentions,
no matter how hard they tried not to,

they left a *bisl*
to us, their *liebchens.*

My Ukranian-Jewish Grandparents and Our Chinese Child's Birth Parents Meet at a Café and Discuss Her Future

Schmuel and Malka and our child's
Chinese birth parents are sipping tea
at a café somewhere between the Pale
of Settlement and central-rural China.

They speak in signs and gestures, swirling
arms like dancers, shaping fingers into figures,
standing up and swaying, contorting bodies
to emphasize some obscure point, even

employing pauses and long silences to further
the conversation. The men gesture:
my grandfather's yarmulke is as black
as I imagine our child's birth father's hair.

The women continue to fill their husband's cups
and stare off into the distance.
The men agree on the major issue:
each will have to sacrifice their darlings,

their children—send them away, across
miles of land and ocean, into a realm further
and more unfamiliar than they could understand
even in their own tongue, a place perhaps

like those faraway and never-never lands
in the stories of each of their childhoods:
palace on a cloud, temple beyond the stars,
Jerusalem or Shangri-la. It's better

to think of that strange country this way
than to ponder the potential dangers—
strangers in strange lands, years of forced labor,
the poverty and destitution they themselves

know something about, each in their own way,

these farmers and peddlers, each of them know
dark to dark. Their gestures are more subtle
and sophisticated now, they even forget

and sometimes break out into their Yiddish
and Mandarin, which sounds as exotic
as a gathering of multicolored birds
singing through the tea's steam.

The bill, which is grief, arrives.
They agree to split it.
They accompany each other to the gate
that opens out into their separate centuries.

Through unfathomable signs, they gesture to meet again.

Tormented Meshugenahs

Where are the crazy tormented sages?

The ones who dervished across the hayfields
and paused to yawp a parable to the cows about the seven
beggars,

that tale layered like an onion,
and when you peel it you wail like the child you still are,
wounded and wonderful?

And where are the wonder rabbis who wandered
all over and off this world,
measuring distance between our dreams and the stars,

the ones who wrote the testaments,
the commentaries on the commentaries,
the interpreters, the ones who exclaimed:

You haven't seen nothing yet!
This world is but preparation!

Those meshugenahs!

Summer harvest, we eat of the soil,
basil into pesto, tomatoes into sauce.

And our prayers: a little table talk, a lot of laughter—

and the children, inhaling their supper, tearing out,
bodies bonkers with they don't know what,

scampering the field to the pond,
searching for koi, jelly fish, frogs, dizzy with this, elated with
that.

In the next world, will we be greeted with white scarf and
crown?
Will we be invited to share in the feast?
Will we speak the language that should have been our own?
Will we reach a companionable silence?

Oh, you so-called rebbes, disclose the secrets only you know,
what the worms are whispering beneath the earth you bow
your bodies toward.
Enter our dreams and reveal the object of our yearnings.

We move from book to garden, from garden to book.

Now is the time to taste the fruit before it enters the fruit,
the way God consulted the Book before creating the world.

Why look deeper into the garment of the moment?

We want to read both testaments, the laws and the love,
the patriarchs and the forgiveness, the silence that Buddha
taught.
We want the dharma and the java, the rebirth and the vegetable
love.
We're topsy-turvey for the duration,

for our daughters placing small apples into the dog's mouth.

See what I mean?
It's like water, isn't it?

It's like the dream we call our life.

This Flickering World

The Synagogue in Oil City, Pennsylvania

The congregation disappears one by one
into another service underground or on top
of the air where there is no trouble

making a minyan like there is here
in this temple above the Allegheny River
and a block from where, less and less,

tankers rattle over the Petroleum Bridge,
carrying their crude. Orthodox,
not allowed to use the phone on this day

of rest, have Frank, the gentile neighbor
with the orange hunting jacket, call up
any Jews still left because you need

at least ten so that each prays
for the entire and not only for the self.
During the Torah portion no longer

the sound of drills, the derricks pumping.
Now the quiet grows with each responsive
chanting, each loss making a little more room

to be filled in by a mysterious God.
The names on the scroll of the dead outnumber
the names called to read from the Book

or carry it on their shoulders around
the tabernacle, singing in the Sabbath.
So many injunctions to lift over their bodies.

The children left with the economy
and will not return. These are the last
generation in a town with no rabbi,

who took another job. And who can blame him,
not wanting to be the one to bury them all,
these final chosen to keep the word here,

where they gather out of habit or a faint
calling in the blood like those birds
who return to the same place the same time

to sing together in their sanctuary
until it is filled, like this town
after the refinery closes, with silence.

Two Dwellings

1: *The Jewish Quarter in Krakow*

On the doorway of a dwelling
beside the synagogue in Krakow, Poland—

an indentation, a space
in the shape of a mezuzah,

what we are commanded
to fasten to our gates

so that each time we arrive
or leave we press

our fingertips to our lips
and touch the one prayer

that will recall us
to our lives. A trespasser

on the threshold, I look both ways
and kiss the emptiness.

2: *Cleveland Heights, Ohio: Miller's Chapel*

Not the main sanctuary, with its white dome
and the choir and the microphone for the rabbi,

but this tiny room in the back of the basement,
some tapestry, the ark, a few scattered chairs,

the same minyan of mourners that gathers in the hour
of first light, shuffling in with their shadows.

On both sides, windows, the surrounding trees,
so when the service calls for them to sing the *Shema*

or the *Kaddish*, they are birds chirping in Hebrew
and the song arises from out of a deep forest.

Just dawn, it is all part of the flickering world.
There are no lights on but the everlasting that shines

on the book open to where they all are at this moment—
old men and women wearing their work clothes,

hurrying their prayers before the day's labor—
this one has to visit her sick husband in intensive care,

that one has to sign a contract for a settlement—
none of them daring to drive from home

to work in a direct line without a detour to God
here, in this out-of-the-way storage room

of yarmulkes and tefillin and tallit, a space
so small each voice is distinguished from the rest.

With the Survivors

At the service in the Rehmuh Synagogue,
the last one left in Krakow, Poland
not a museum, across from kosher-
style cafes and trained klezmers,

the dozen ancient men don't rise
at the appropriate passage in the liturgy,
they don't read responsively with the rabbi
or follow along in the prayer book.

They *kibitz*, as if their gossip
and news were more significant
than whatever God is telling them.
In the back pew I attempt to follow

the Hebrew above the Polish-Yiddish
muttering of these men in stained
sweaters, untucked shirts, ties
barely knotted as if they had no one

to dress them. Suddenly, the *Shema:*
The Lord is Our God, the Lord is one,
the prayer you must remember after
you have forgotten everything else.

The ark opens, as if from a wind.
All at once each worshipper grips
their seat's edge, forearms quivering,
struggling to lift their body's weight

of resistance to confront the Holy Book.
No one hoists it out of the sanctum
and heaves it above his shoulders,
no one bears it around the sanctuary

for the congregation to touch it
with their tallits or caress its scroll
with their kissed prayer books.
Who was it closed the curtains?

We retire to a back table set
with cake and vodka, shot glasses
filled to the brim, recite in cracked
voices the blessing for the fruit

of the vine, throw back the clear fire.
Over our thin slice, we chant words
for the earth, the morning liquor
lightening my head, the dusty air swirling

the table a few inches above the ground,
the room tilting, spinning, these faces
floating on the air's surface—flat, as if
what they witnessed froze their expressions.

One beside me—hair tussled, skin rough
like coarse paper, speaks, half Yiddish,
half English, shrugs his right arm: *East.*
To Ruskie. Vork. The vodka goes around.

Someone murmurs: *Shabbat shalom.*

The Jewish Quarter in Budapest

1. The Orthodox Synagogue

In this former Jewish neighborhood,
where Kazinczy Street curves
hardly wider than an alley,

in a Sunday quiet, hidden in its own
shadows, sun climbing its back,
across the street a gate opened

to a courtyard, a mother and child
sweeping up a cobbled walkway.
Under Reconstruction, a sign says,

near a partially covered open door where
a heavy-set man hauling an electric cord
waves me inside through mounds of plaster,

pieces of stones and lumber. Upstairs,
in the woman's section, tarped pews.
Soft morning light is muted through stained glass.

The chandeliers are sheeted and drooping
lopsided from the ceiling over the sanctuary,
shaped like wrapped bells. In front,

two workers crouch on a scaffold, delicately
etching Jewish stars with blue paint on thin brushes.
Something is putting back this house

of worship piece by piece, star by star.
They don't look like angels. They chatter back
and forth, sometimes climb down to take

a piss or bring up more paint to continue
their task on this eastern wall above
the bimah and the holy scrolls.

If they drop a brush, they don't raise
its silken hairs to their lips the way a yarmulke
must be kissed each time it falls.

The sanding, the molding, the staining,
the Sabbath Bride. In the loose wires
and sawdust, the Lord is One.

2. At the Kosher Restaurant

Where you can sit elbow to elbow
with ancient rabbis in beards
and sidelocks, the guidebook says

but, instead, there are cats in the courtyard
behind the synagogue. They scatter
at my approach, experts in survival.

Upstairs the empty dining area
and, beyond, the narrow kitchen
where a tiny man, ancient, rabbinical,

black suit and black yarmulke
that covers his whole head, sits alone
at a small table against the window,

sipping soup from a white bowl.
His face is cracked parchment,
back hunched over as if

he's been carrying the Torah
above his head during all the years
of darkness. He's so small,

perhaps he survived in a refrigerator,
a cabinet, the ark of the holy scrolls,
maybe he folded himself up into a word,

a single letter, it's possible
he became the hardly distinguishable
silence between the call and the response.

I pause at the doorway and stare
the way, at the museum, I studied
photographs of the round-ups

and the trains, recognized shofars
and circumcision knives behind
protective glass. He won't pose

as I snap the camera but stays
his place, sipping his soup, as if
I was the one who didn't exist.

The House of Sages

I pause before the House of Sages,
beside the boarded-up synagogue,
on my walk down East Broadway

toward the river for relief
from the heat's tidal wave.
Founded in 1922, the slab stone says,

the year of my father's birth.
The white sign above the caged
door announces in Hebrew

the Polish shtetl of its origin.
Near the bold lock and intercom
a spray of white paint:

swirls and loops like lopsided
hearts and question marks
and the street's fevered talk.

Through the cracked window
men in black were poring
dusty faces over pages spread

open like stilled wings,
quivering bodies revealed
in this afternoon glare shafting

the lower East Side. I wanted
to enter there, to assume
the white robe and crown, to bow

down low before the open Ark
and touch the book
with my scarf and place my fingers

to my lips and kiss there.
I wanted all of this, to arrive
and hear my name called,

son of my mother and father, in the first
language and all the silence after.
I stood in the sidewalk's fire.

The gate opened. A bearded shadow
appeared and I stole inside
before it closed like a cloud behind me.

I peeked into the sanctuary
of the sacred and a sage
was reading a newspaper

the way my father or I myself
relaxed at table, long legs
stretched out on the dark oak,

feet crossed. Another
was solving a crossword puzzle,
inquiries in the holy tongue.

What questions down?
What questions across?
Were the answers printed

in the next life? A few
were bending their torsos
down and up, up and down,

as if lettering with their bodies
some unfathomable word
or testing out a new law of physics:

if you rub flesh with air, a spark.
Soon, first one then another
turned toward my direction,

all staring, eyes fixed, curious
at my intrusion. Should they touch
their foreheads to the eastern wall

or call the police? Briefly all the noise
of New York became one word
which filled the room, our only world.

Singer Among the Pigeons

There are laws against you.
How you shit over everything—
noisemakers, nuisances, stalkers

of rooftops and statues, stealing
underfoot, gathering in gangs,
subject to regulations, legal

poisons, experimental research.
But then: *Who knows?* he said,
your spokesman, your messiah—

in the next generation, perhaps
we'll all return as hungry pigeons,
feeding you on the corner of Broadway

and West 96th on his daily walk
to the corner table at the café
where he met his characters

for a vegetarian lunch—potatoes
and knish, a glass of cold tea—
you perched in gutters, waiting.

He was reliable as the faded
bathrobe and shabby slippers
he wrote in, typing his stories

straight through, as dependable
as his destroyed streets of Bilgoray,
the houses with low roofs covered

with tiles and moss, the rooms
of his own house, the bookshelves,
all the holy books, each word and letter,

as faithful as the Yiddish scholar and peddlers,
the dialect he spoke to you in, the *shmegegge,*
convinced you'd understand him, the *putz,*

speaking in a dead tongue to rejected birds.
God's creatures, he called you, an odd bird
himself with his flappy ears and wide eyes,

pale cheeks and beaked nose, awkward,
like his heroes, a bit of a shlemiel, like Gimpel,
ugly, like you, a luftmensch living on air,

his bald head, you all agreed, a good target.
Once, one of you landed on his hat: *a pigeon*
wouldn't land on just anyone, he asserted—

they can distinguish a Jewish writer
and wouldn't do anything to hurt him.
That's the way he thought, this believer.

Some of you might even be his ancestors,
his grandparents the rabbis or his mother—
though it was forbidden—the Talmudic scholar,

his father the wise man of Krochmalna Street.
Some of you may have been all the Jews
he left behind, the ones he couldn't save,

and now, perhaps, one of you—which one,
among the tens of thousands scattered
and hungry throughout this city?—

coos in a language so stubborn it will not die.

Night of the Broken Glass

Glass lasts a million years.
Where are these remnants?

If they could speak, would they voice
the history of their shattering?

Was the glass sorted and washed
and crushed and melted

and molded into bottles?
These slivers, where do they reside?

Can each shard represent
a fragment, sharp and fragile,

of a scattered soul? Isn't
a soul similar to glass, hard

and brittle, transparent and
translucent, vulnerable,

easily cracked, as they are here,
burst like razored shrapnel,

on this storefront sidewalk on
Thursday, November 10, 1938?

Pedestrians, overcoated, marching,
as if on command, on their way to work,

gripping briefcases, pausing,
glancing briefly at the jagged map

of emptiness that, only a few hours ago,
was the window display that blocks of granite

for repairing roads were heaved through
to shape into a new country of hatred.

A window can be a mirror.
When, in the dead of night,

as the citizens approached
Lichenstein Taschen and Co.,

did they recognize, in their reflection,
their own shadowed and contorted shapes?

And so the destruction began.

Children's Holocaust Museum

Jerusalem

This is what being blind is like:
at first, absolute black, a theater
before the screen flashes—

you negotiate the narrow hallway,
one hand trembling on the railing,
the other held out to avoid accident—

then: one candle, two, a few more,
the way the first stars will clarify
as the sky slightly darkens—

the more you look, the more appear
until the sky is full of them, a universe
of candles spread out in each direction,

and you are at its center.
You can never count them
or see them all at once.

It must be done with mirrors,
you think, a building this small
could not contain so much light,

and you come to understand:
one and a half million out of six,
this you know, but how many millions

from these, and these again, countless.

Drying the Torah

for Cantor Michal and Chris Hood

Because the synagogue pipes burst
in the coldest part of the winter,
causing mildew in the holy ark, the Torah
became damp, edges curled like dried
leaves, stitched sinews loosened
between sheets of sheepskin, dabs of ink—
prepared ages ago from soot, tree sap
and honey, dissolved in gallnut juice, scribed
with the feather of a goose, its quill
a reed and not a weapon of destruction—
bleeding through the parchment.
And the two women lift its heaviness,
delicately remove the silver crown
and breastplate, unfasten its pointer,
slip off the velvet robe, unscroll
and spread out all five books across
the length of the sanctuary, 304,
805 letters exposed and revealed
to the open air, from *In the beginning*
to the death of Moses, *whom the Lord knew*
face to face. They press their own faces
close to the surface as they can, closer,
without breaking the law of touching it,
inhale deeply the animal flesh: *Smells*
like my horse, says one. *Like soil*, says
the other. They whisper how it will lay there
overnight in the sanctuary, freed finally
from its closet where it is condemned
to straighten up at attention until
the curtain parts and the congregation
rises—and for once it will be released
from all that worship, all that praise,
all that chanting and bowing and chanting

and bowing. Alone in the silent dark
   of its healing, will it remember when
   it was torn and spit upon? Will it recall
when it was set on fire? Or will it dream
   of all those lovers embracing its body as if
   they were quivering on a tottering earth
all the days and nights of their lives?

Jewing Him Down

At the meeting, Natalie, the go-to gal for anything volunteer related, was describing her conversation with the grocery store owner. We're trying to raise more money for a new playground, and she's been hard at work organizing fundraisers. They're talking raffle: $5.00 a ticket, winner take all—in this case, huge pounds of meat, plus a freezer to store it in. And meat's no joke in southern Venango county, rural, poorest region in the state. We're meeting in the art room of the elementary school—crouching on child-sized chairs pulled up against the low table, Natalie and Tammy's kids drawing on the chalkboard. "So I was talking to the guy" —Natalie wants to get the best price she can—"you know, trying to jew him down..."

And suddenly the room froze and though her lips kept moving it felt like all the words that followed were like the way wheels keep spinning when the car has already spilled over the side of the hill.

I like Natalie. The school would fall apart without her. And the kids need a new playground. The wheels slowed down to a standstill.

A Minyan Plus One

was taken from us on the Shabbat,
the most joyous of the holidays,
the only holy day even God Himself

•

celebrates, the emulation of Eden,
the day of completion. Before
they could perform the service, before

•

they could take their seats and begin
the prayers, before the ark opened
and the Torah revealed,

•

before they could rise and sway
and chant their portion, the book
opened like wings in their steady hands,

•

though they know the blessings by heart.
I didn't know them, but I knew them
in the way we know those raised,

•

no matter where we originated,
in the same beliefs our ancestors
inherited all the way back into

•

those mysterious origins,
those stories of creation and exile,
of miracles and complicated kings,

•

of commandments and wisdoms—
"welcome the stranger"—
spread across the millennium.

•

We suffer the same persecutions,
celebrate the same triumphs, chant,
in the same order, the blessings,

•

hour after hour, holiday after holiday,
generation after generation,
Torah portion after Torah portion.

Before that week's Torah portion,
a minyan plus one was taken.
When they would have once again

heard the story of when Abraham,
our first Patriarch of Chutzpah,
approached and argued with the Lord:

"Will you sweep away the righteous
with the wicked?" And the Lord answered:
"For the sake of ten, I will not destroy it."

And so, as on other days, on that day—
He did. He allowed the wicked
to sweep away the righteous.

And when the Lord had finished
speaking with Abraham, He left.
And took a minyan plus one.

And Abraham returned home.

for the eleven victims of the Tree of Life Synagogue shootings in Pittsburgh, PA on October 27, 2018

Saying the Kaddish for Those Who Have No One to Say the Kaddish

At the appropriate
portion of the service—
even if not recalling
a loved one—those
who are able rise
and recite
the memorial prayer
for the millions
for whom there is
no one to mourn,
this prayer that
has no mention
of the loved one,
but only *glorified*
and sanctified be
thy Name and *may*
God speedily establish
His kingdom in
our lifetime. And
so it applies to those
who passed away
in the fullness
of age or untimely
perished in the midst
of their days and work's
completion, before
all their offerings
were received
and passed on
and properly blessed.
And so we say Kaddish
for them, and for all
who would have chanted
after them, who,
standing and swaying,

bending knees
and balancing the book
open to its proper page,
are now us,
though we know
the words by heart.

The Service

Her Conversion

I make myself pure
in this preparation room,
scrape away mascara,
eye shadow, lipstick,

brush and floss
every last bit of crumb,
swab my nose and ears,
as the law demands.

The attendant lays a path
of towels on the floor
from the sink to the mikvah,
the ritual bath, as if I

were the celebrity and so
even the soles of my feet
won't touch the tile once out
of their earthly shoes.

Naked under my new robe,
I walk into the holy chamber—
a small room of stone
with a pool of warm water

where orthodox women purify
after their time of bleeding
and no men are present.
Now is my immersion.

I plunge my whole body
without touching any wall
so that I'm floating
as in the womb

of my first birth.
To immerse
is to be sanctified,
to submerge and disappear

the way a moon hides
in the shadow of its planet.
I am being koshered,
like a knife that sliced

through the unclean.
The voice of the rabbi
resonates in this echo-
chamber the way the voice

of God spoke from down
the mountain or from out
of the bush—without
form, seeping like

the living waters
through these copper pipes
from an unidentifiable source.
I am where it doesn't feel

like anywhere else,
suspended, listening
to words that glisten
like grain—I glean them

bit by bit, as in a field of barely,
worthy before witnesses,
sustained and wet
in my choice, steadfastly given.

The Last Torah Reader

has taken his voice
— more of a croak than a croon—
and his wisdom of the letters

to chant among the sages.
He wasn't a learned man—
a common laborer, rather,

just another member
of the congregation,
who became, in the absence

of a real rabbi, a shaman
of the secret signs
and mysterious marks

of the Masoretic text—
the accents and niggunim
and tropes, saying—

like a bearded chazzan
trained across the centuries—
each syllable according to its ritual,

the accents and intonations,
deciphering the florid vowel-less script,
swaying us through the service

in spite of ourselves.
He was our Ezra, as described
in the Book of Nehemiah, chanting

as if we just returned from exile,
taking on the obligation
that passed from tongue to tongue

for who knows how long,
performing the required mitzvah,
guiding the congregation

in that week's portion of law.
We'd rise and he'd roar out
those passages from the open scroll:

off-key, out of tune, tone pitched
beyond the sanctuary and across
the street. One of the Greatest Generation,

he was among those who liberated Dachau:
They had nowhere to go, he grieved.
Then he returned to Butler, Pennsylvania

to begin his long marriage
and home improvement business
and good citizenship because for such

a position the chief qualification
is a measureless spirit, resounding
in his cracked voice our word of God.

for Leonard Abes

The Rabbi in Retirement

At the coffee shop the rabbi
who held his palms in the air
over my head and announced
that I was a man

bows over a table by the window,
reading the sports section.

What would the Talmudists say?

Would Rashi peer over
his eighty-five-year-old body
and wonder why he's not davening
with the mourners?

                    Or would
he allow him to rest at long last
from the Great Factory of the Eternal?

On the Day of Atonement, he'd rail
against our lethargy, our paralysis,
he'd speak sparks, his voice
enflaming the sanctuary, a violent rage,

fists beating the pulpit, spraying
spit into the trapped air,
bellowing how in our comfortable lives

we will watch our gardens wither
and our faces will be faces of flame,

his very own flock falling from the faith,
lukewarm in love and labor, moderate
in our passions, indifferent to the poor
of the spirit and the flesh, which is grass.

When he paused it seemed the synagogue
would shake and he would reveal the names
written in invisible ink and signed
and sealed by an unseen hand in the Great Book.

Isaiah sits across from him
as he sips his coffee and folds
the paper to the financial page.

Hillel, silent so as not to disturb,
sweeps up in a circle around his throne.

The Sofer

Because of the frigid cold,
a pipe burst and leaked
even into the holy Ark,

the Torah removed, scrolls
spread out on the long table,
sunlight filtering through stained glass.

The sofer, his eyes so close,
almost kissing the parchment,
scrutinizes the scriptures

for stains, smudges, erasures,
along each stitched section,
down and up the 304, 805 letters

complicated as roses,
clearing smeared backgrounds,
inking besmirched words,

sweeping plaster dust,
making certain no letters touch.
If the error involves God's name,

he removes the whole parchment
and buries it like the beloved dead.
He says: *Each letter has to be kosher.*

I'm doing this for the sake
of the holiness of what I'm doing,
this black-coated ghost

from a world we thought lost,
this scientist of the sacred, ordained
to calculate our errors and present us the bill.

Hasidim in New Square, New York Hear Carp Speaking Hebrew

Latest miracle, back of a local fish market:
A carp opened its mouth and declared:
I am the soul of a dead childless Hasid!
I was sent to do good deeds on earth!
It spoke first to its executioner, Luis
Nivelo, one of the non-believers, just
as it was about to be gutted: *The fish*
is talking! Nivelo screamed. Zalmen
Rosen, his boss, rushed into the room
and the fish, in the ancient tongue, confirmed—
Yes! I'm the soul of a departed Jew,
come back to relieve your burdens,
to heal your sick of heart, to give strength
to the weary—then slid into the fish pile.
Attempts to recover it were fruitless,
one carp looking so much like another,
the way they can slip and slide until lost
among the school. When the workers called,
in their ache to re-affirm, why didn't it respond?
Why didn't it raise its voice out of the heap
of its inarticulate brethren and distinguish itself
again? So it was sold with the rest.
Some believe it was as the parting of the Red Sea,
as the giving of the commandments.
Reports spread: a carp spoke God's word.
The Messiah is coming, such was the rumor.
The local rabbi decreed: to honor this wonder
everyone should not eat carp for a week.

The Service

And with a man you shall not lie as with a woman…
—Leviticus 18:22

Despite the passages in *Leviticus*
which cause him a consternation
he doesn't know what to do with,
Ben embraces the tradition—

wearing not only the yarmulke
but the knotted fringes dangling
from his shirt: he touches them,
as it is written, to remember

the mitzvahs and do them,
and so always in the grocery store
or the laundromat he's noticed
and commented on, his body

a Torah passage surrounded
by interpretations by his fellow citizens,
the tradition he's turned to
and learned the language so thoroughly

he can read from the scripture
and teach Talmud to the Christians.
Once, after a holiday celebration,
a stranger appeared, unwashed,

black beard unkempt, eyes glassy,
stumbling, stammering.
We backed away. Ben approached,
offered him cake and lemonade:

How do we know he's not Elijah?
For the diminishing congregation
he mows in the summer, shovels in the winter,
cleans the sanctuary and the bathrooms,

the recreation hall and the rabbi's office,
interprets the week's portion for the monthly newsletter,
leads the service when the rabbi is away.
Is the ladder needed to change the eternal light?—

this appointed one assuring the shul
is kosher and the worship can commence
according to the commandments:
What a blessing! Serving the House of Hashem!

If it weren't for Leviticus 18 and 20, he adds—
to himself, his silent petition, his abomination.

Her Voice

I deliver a box of matzo to the only trailer
with a mezuzah nailed to the doorframe.
She rents on her fixed income from a trucker

and his wife, Rhesa, in Clintonville, PA, county
of Amish and the rural poor, county of non-zoning,
of cars in various states of repair on front lawns

and roaming Dobermanns, of rusted-out tractors
and burn piles, where the local politicos
always say is a "perfect place for toxic waste,"

backdropped as it is by Interstate 80. Nights
truckers' beams crisscross her living room
and she accuses Rhesa of flashlighting

her privacy to catch the poodles she calls
her children at shitting on the carpet.
Weak heart, bipolar, not-yet-forty, boxes

piled from ceiling to floor her fortification,
stuffed with bargain-basement garage sale
clothes, books, dishes, tchotchkes

she makes her life's accumulation.
And when the rooms fill up with dust and mold
she moves them with her dogs and medication.

Across the road the Amish farm. Mornings
she watches children in black walk toward
the school their parents built, watches late afternoons

their return. And the perennial black buggy
and the stocky taut workhorses, their muscles
shimmering with heat as they furrow their dignity

into the soil, the smallest boy following the father,
who wrapped around his shoulders the leather tefillin
of the plow, up and across and down and across

the rows, the light slanting across the field,
blazing their horizon the color of fire or God's face
on their daily routine of returning back to the world.

Does she wonder if this is how her great-grandparents,
also orthodox and curiosities, balanced their lives,
bunched together, working their land with their strange rules

and eating habits, their mysterious worship?
This is too far away from any public agency.
On the first of the month when the check arrives

we take her shopping and on Passover
to the synagogue fifty miles away in Butler,
where she sits off to the side and her lips move.

And only Elijah can distinguish her voice.

Albert Einstein at the Soup Kitchen

Do I look like anyone? he asks,

as he swoops the long spoon into the peas,
lifts it a few inches
and holds it steady to pour
onto the tray of the next famished mouth,
shouts to George for more
as his supply empties down.

I'm the bread and donut man
in this assembly line of volunteers
who gather for our three-hour
of weekly service and socialism:

Jose the finger-pointing Filipino
who pours the punch and repeats:
The wages of sin is death
and only reads *Paradise* from the *Comedy*,

for his description of heaven, he says, *and light;*

Jake the Buddhist, who scrapes the dishes
as they are returned, saves whatever
appears untouched for someone else's

insatiable hunger;
        Sal, who tells me he was on the other side
of the line, meaning he was one of the thousand
who form every morning single-file around this Church
of the Apostles, up 9th Avenue and around

28th Street,
        like the snake, he chants,
looking out the window beyond Crack Park,

cursed above the beasts of the city
to eat dust all the days of its life.

And their eyes are filled with dust,
        drugged and sleepy,
bodies stiff from sidewalk cardboard sofas.

The peaman, it turns out, looks like Albert Einstein,
the shaggy white hair and white mustache,
pronounced nose and dark sad eyes.

I'm an actor, he explains. *They pay me to look like the genius.*

He shows me his card: *E=mc2.*
Equity equals many characters,

and I'm honored to be near even the resemblance of the man—
not because I understand relativity
and the contradicting theories of light,

but because of how steady he is with a spoon,
filling each helping to the brim,
as if each portion should be equal

and abundant.

I Would Be a Priest

I would be a Kohanim,
a descendent of Moses and Aaron,
of the tribe of Levites,

and light the seven candles,
and transport the holy Ark
across the wilderness,

and be the first to be called
to the book, and recite
the priestly blessings—oh,

I would give up my house
and property to perform
the duty of holiness,

all day and throughout the night,
because *the Lord God Himself*
would be my only inheritance—

but I am content to be among
the congregation of common stock,
another voice in a chorus of voices,

standing and sitting and standing
and sitting through the service
until the final benediction, then

strolling in loose clothes and tennis shoes
to my small yard and listen
to whatever music arises out of the silence

until dusk turns to dark.

Ruth Bader Ginsberg

Mothers should prefer their daughters
careful, cautious, skeptical, unapologetic,
unaffected by fashion, an advocate for their committed
causes, Kowtowing to no one, unafraid to dissent
or to be appropriately difficult, mothers should prefer
daughters to know the history of daughters,
of those daughters without whom they would not
have the wisdom to become women,
citizens of a republic that would not
be a republic without them,
that without them it would be the sham
it often threatens to become, mothers
prefer their daughters to be discerning
in deciding, *to consider a field before they buy it.*

Bernie Could Have Been My Father

for Bernie Levine 1929-2013

Bernie would drive all the way to Youngstown
for a few pounds of corned beef and rye bread,
the kind with seeds we'd consume with onion rings
and Dr. Brown's black cherry soda. He wasn't
my father, but he could have been, I could have
learned my bar mitzvah lesson in the backseat
of his Lincoln Town Car on the way to the track.
I could have witnessed how he'd play the numbers
between customers of L and L Glass and Paint Co.,
in Butler, Pennsylvania, and on the Sabbath,
I could have listened as he chanted
the tropes of the Torah portion, tone deaf but
accurate, holding the synagogue together,
a synagogue himself, if a man could embody
a congregation, and Bernie did, his heart
so devoted to this struggling house of God,
its roof dripping during the difficult part
of the service, the part where you have to stand
and read silently so that only God will hear you—
Bernie had that fixed, too, he had a number to call
out of his infinite list of numbers of plumbers
and painters and general cleaners he'd pay
off the books, this "unofficial mayor of Butler,"
his son—who I could have been—called him,
because he never went anywhere he wasn't known,
even in some roadside diner in South Carolina
someone would be at the next table who'd
recognize him from somewhere, some roulette
wheel in Atlantic City, maybe he saw Bernie
pass out $100 bills to each of his sons
and his sons' friends and to all his grandchildren
and maybe even strangers because Bernie
wanted everyone to have a good time, his body
now lowered into the earth he faithfully mowed

and tended, surrounded by the congregation
he made sure would continue—
and we will continue, Bernie, you can bet on it.

One Continuous Flow

for Eric Levine, 1964-2022

Mr. Inoperable

Mr. President-of-our-Synagogue,
Mr. Cigar-Smoking, Beer-Drinking
Steelers-Watching, Torah-Chanting,

Mr. Fix-The-Leak-Before-the-Scrolls
Are-Ruined, Mr. Famous-Gambler
of-Atlantic City, Mr. Without-Whom-

We-Wouldn't-Even-Hear-a-Still-Small-Voice.
And for your faith to the word this reward.
Now your yarmulke is transducers attached

with adhesive bandages connected to wires
plugged into a battery the size of a book
we hope is sacred. On a Sunday morning

I sat beside your king-sized bed
and you said you didn't sleep well, and so
the day would go badly for you.

All I want is to sit on the porch,
smoke a cigar and watch the game.
You pulled the cover back to reveal

your tremendous hairy body
that you somehow managed to rise up
to its mountainous height.

Shabbat, Late Afternoon

Astounding, when you passed—
on the Shabbat, like Joseph,
Moses and David—late afternoon,

the beauty of the hour,
mid-summer, just before harvest,
day of rest, day of completion—

an honor, it is written, not only
for the observant here,
but for the souls in the hereafter,

righteous son, righteous father,
righteous citizen, righteous friend,
righteous worshipper, the way

you couldn't, during services
and on High Holy Days, remain
in your seat—you'd get out of your pew

and stroll around the sanctuary,
whispering to a congregant here,
shaking a congregant's hand there.

When we were lacking a rabbi,
you conducted the service yourself,
leading us in the prayers

in your homespun Hebrew.
On holy days you'd count
to yourself how many members

in attendance, lamenting its diminishing,
determined to hold us together,
the way you watched your father

worry about the plumbing.
It was a family affair, this House
of God, this only remaining synagogue

between Erie and Pittsburgh
in our state's rust belt. Though
in Job we read that our days are fixed,

why did the God you served—
driving at the end of each work week
to Pittsburgh for kosher meat—

strike you down so suddenly,
so young, before the synagogue picnic,
the Days of Awe?

We're still here, you'd claim.
We're still plugging away.
It's a blessing.

The Last Mikvah

How calm and thin, having lost
the weight of your illness,
your body as polished as ivory

overlaid with sapphires.
So goes the *Song of Songs*
we sing over you

in our cracked voices
as we perform the sacraments
and make the profane sacred.

We recite the prayer
for you to forgive us
any unintentional indiscretions

as I ask for your forgiveness
for any inappropriate words,
then slowly pour

the water over you,
like a well-moistened garden
for this final mikvah,

starting at the head down
to the toes and back again,
your legs *pillars of marble*

set upon foundations
of fine gold, the way,
our rabbi eulogized,

you were a pillar of our congregation,
like the pillar of cloud to lead us
and a pillar of fire to light our way.

We dry you and clothe you
in the white apparel of royalty:
the linen pants and shirt, the kittel,

which has no pockets.
Where, I wonder,
will you keep the coins

you'll earn in God's casino,
dealing the blackjack
you learned from your father

and taught diligently to your son?
And the matches
to light the cigars

friends will place on your chest—
beside your tallis, snipped,
as you are no longer required

to follow the laws, of one tassel—
before sealing you into eternity for good?
I was mesmerized, you'd said.

I loved the spirituality of it all.

Our Scriptures

Among the Scribes

Didn't they tell you, all those sages,
that the promised land is this moment?

Here, now, this late summer air, this dew-drenched field,
this thin filament of gossamer between an apple tree and an
   apple tree?
The almost unnoticeable blue jay feather in the unmown grass?

Remember when you were Moses?

Remember when you couldn't speak
and they spit on you and you garbled and slurred your words?

Always you were singular as the swallowtail
losing itself in the goldenrod profusion.

Remember when you were Whitman?
Twirling a leaf of grass?—like this morning:

coffee, beside your wife,
in the shadow of the shade garden and a sassafras,
drops of tree-rain dripping patterns on your page,
hydrangeas streaked with the pink of their next incarnation,
the children picking pears, filling their baskets with silliness.

History and the future leave you suspended
like a hummingbird's pause.

A leaf falls.
Who ordered these distractions?

The rain tells you one thing, the silence another,
but that traitor, summer, that shameful lover,
gathers back to itself its sweetness, its light, reclaiming its juices,

so you want to sing poems deep
as those psalms chanted with exact pronunciation to the text,
the precise cantillations, the pauses and stresses,
and—beautiful, the way that swallowtail now dips and dives
its yellow into the yellow of the sunflowers.

Are you adding to the law?
Are you composing your holy writ?
Don't we all want to translate each moment into the eternal?

Isn't this your flowering time?
Aren't you robed in royalty?
And shouldn't every word be a fiery contribution?

And aren't even you, a meshuggenah from Cleveland, among
the scribes?

Moses Had His Burning Bush

Our daughters stepping off the school bus
        and charging full-tilt across

the sweetness of the just-mown hayfield
        toward the blossoming dogwood

breaks the heart precisely in two,
        even as the songbirds sweeten

our seconds, even as the white petals
        linger a little longer into dusk

until we get it right. Are we getting it right?
        Are we swirling according to instructions?

Moses had his Sinai and we have
        the brief life of this dogwood,

which, if it wasn't so alone among
        the maples and the oaks,

if it wasn't so embarrassed by its beauty,
        perhaps we wouldn't be so distracted

by those two geese racketing up the sky.
        If the breeze wasn't so soft

across the familiar skin of our faces,
        if the spring itself wasn't so unreliable

in its arrivals and departures,
        perhaps something could be said,

something simple would announce itself
        and the evening would unfold like any other—

useful and dignified, disappearing into
        wherever the dogwood leaves disappear into.

Moses had his burning bush and we have
        our dogwood. Would he trade

his dividing of the great sea for these children
        parting the clover in their abandon?

His slow tongue for their dogwood song?

Our Scriptures

after Yehuda Amichai

1

You are my Torah and Talmud,
My written and oral testaments.

I perform my midrash
All over your body, dusk into dark—

Rain constant on the slate roof.
Our love is the small text

Inside a circle of commentaries,
Each stroke of the thigh a passage

Interpreted by Rashi, consulted
By the rabbis for thousands of years.

2

Our bodies are the Torah scrolls
Rolled together

And the congregation rises
When the rabbi lifts us out of the ark

And hoists us above his head
And carries us around the synagogue,

Each congregant touching our parchment
With their kissed tallits and prayer books.

And the rabbi places us on the lectern
And unscrolls us to the proper portion

Of our passage. And the chanting
And the love cries are one.

In the School of J

The way we stroll around the garden
of an early spring dusk,

God walked in the cool
of the evening.

If I could choose,
I would labor in the school of J,

those scribes who wrote all the good parts
of Genesis, Exodus, Numbers—

to be one of their lesser servants,
among those who water their camels,

fill their wine jugs,
slaughter and shave and scrape

the sheepskins into parchment,
fashion their pointed reeds into pens,

prepare their ink with charcoal,
water, and gallnut juice,

and, though it is certainly forbidden,
hide behind the gate

and watch my scribe,
who all her life studied for just this:

composing the story of how Jacob,
after watering Laban's flock, kissed Rachel–

and wept out loud.

Isaiah at Rest

All day I've been reading Isaiah,
who I imagine to be ordinary,
in love with a woman who like you

grows and then cooks the vegetables
and only cares about a happy life.
Ye shall be confounded for the gardens

that ye have chosen doesn't apply to her,
he meant it in a more rhetorical way.
And when he arrives home late, his voice

gone, his throat aching, feet scarred
and scratched from all the hard roads,
she puts in front of him a bowl

of last season's harvest: potatoes, tomatoes,
carrots, onions, basil, fennel, dill.
It tastes in his mouth not as the tongue

of fire devours the stubble
or *as the dry grasses sinketh down in the flame*
but more flavorful of their earth

than the live coals that touched his lips
and took away his iniquities. He loosens
the girdle of righteousness from his waist,

and takes off completely the girdle
of faithfulness from his loins,
being in any case more full

of the knowledge of his sources.
All flesh is grass, he whispers
into her ear, and the smell

of his fiery breath
makes her asks him to whisper it
again.

Kaddish for Kafka

On this almost hundredth anniversary of your death
I woke early, walked toward where the light
was emerging, beyond the railroad tracks, the signals,
the crossbars descending to hold back the traffic.

I squinted into the oncoming engine and counted
train cars. I failed. They kept disappearing and more
arriving, an endless stream, as if it were standing still,
like your Great Wall of China, what I can't see

to the end of, as I've already lost track
of its beginnings. Near your end you were preparing
for a journey to the promised land, learning Hebrew,
studying Talmud, living with an orthodox woman,

hoping, you wrote, though in your stories the word
"Jew" was never mentioned, to return back to the fold.
Near the end you became your art and your art became
you, ninety pounds, on your deathbed, unable

to swallow, reading the final proofs of "The Hunger Artist,"
your voice a squeak, like one of your mouse folk,
the ironies flowering like the deep bruise bleeding
out of your lung. The ironies! Berlin! 1924!

Food impossible, the evil arising from the air
you couldn't breathe. And while you were studying
the tractates and writing, in one sitting, about the beast
who will break through the burrow, another vegetarian,

almost your age, was in his own cage, also writing
about Jews as cockroaches, as moles, as dogs, as mice.
At Auschwitz I saw a brown suitcase behind
a glass case with your last name on it, the same name

printed on sugar packets and café signs
in your hometown beside a clown with your face
elongated and wide elephant ears—Kafka,
did any of it help? The vegetarianism, the nudism,

the Zionism, the Fletcherism, the seances, the anarchism,
the Accident Insurance, the engagements, the insomnia,
the headaches, the sanitaria, the gardening, the friendship
with Max, the passion for Milena, the desire to be a waiter

in the holy land, the solitude, the silence, the possibilities
for peace in the human heart, the writing, the writing? It
came. As you knew it would, the torture device
inscribing the sin of being alive on six million souls.

Near the end, the very end, though you couldn't digest,
you ate strawberries and cherries and, though you couldn't
  speak,
whispered, spitting blood into your spittoon, for Dora and
  Robert
to drink beer at your bedside. Did the Judaism help?

As a child, during the prayer service for the dead,
you thought something indecent was occurring and when
the Ark of the Covenant was opened you were reminded
of a shooting gallery—the Torah, Holy of Holies, was

a doll without a head. You hoped you'd never get called
to read from it. When, over your coffin, the rabbi recited
the Kaddish, you stayed, according to reports, where you were.
I say it now, to myself, in the silence you'd prefer.

It's All Possible

for Riad Saleh Hussein

Like a sudden explosion or an attack of the heart,
Your poems arrive from Aleppo, that broken country.

Deaf, mute, handsome, "expansive," I'm told,
"Like Whitman, with an affection for alcohol, and women—a
poetry star."

Until you were tortured, imprisoned, the psychic scars
penetrating deeper,
Then dying, one source claims, of "negligence," and another:
"induced by heartbreak."

Your friends found you alone in your apartment curled on your
bed,
Shivering, hallucinating, begging for a sip of water.

Riad, no one in my country has heard of you.
But here you are: beautiful in this charcoal drawing:

Hair black and thick like Lorca's, sculpted face, eyes dark,
Serious and focused at some nearby disaster,

Diving into your ocean of images: birds, bombs—
*Poor Syria like a bone between the teeth of a dog/a knife in the
hand of a surgeon.*

Riad, in the original, your words travel from right to left,
From your Middle East to my Middle West.

Can this translation give you back the voice you heeded in your
soul's privacy?
You wanted to build a room for a thousand friends.

No end of your wants—

A pocket full of bells; an earthquake of wisdom; clouds under the bed.

Riad, I try to hallucinate with you, to know those erupting rhythms.
But what do I—raised in another scripture,

Our people enemies cursing each other even
Onto the next generations—have to do with you?

That's what I would inquire, if we could sit in my small study,
Sipping tea in the light turning to dark turning to dream

That says it's all possible.
Riad, you wanted *to plough the galaxy,*

To live for all the dead, to place a river in the prison.
When, eyes closed, you were smoking a cigarette, did your angels ascend?

Little amounts of surprises.
Which I write down now, after you.

Darwish and Amichai Reading in Heaven

for Saleh Razzouk

So let's be an open hand,
one of them says, *offering our time*
to the Gods.

The other responds:

Even a fist was an open palm
with five fingers.

And it goes on
like this, year after year, age
after age, these two souls hovering,

indistinguishable in the light,

reciting their spirit selves one
after the other, no longer grieving

their respective exiles,

the breath of their words
shaping the winds
across the deserts
of their homeland,

which is the same homeland,

and now they recite together,

each listening hard
to the other's language.

Yehuda Halevi's Journey to the Holy Land

In Toledo we sat at a small round table
  beside a rose garden and the synagogue,
  our children grouchy from the long walk and the heat—
I wanted to bump into your ghost
  as you chanted that your heart was in the east.
  I wanted to hear your songs of praise,
drinking wine with the Arab poets, composing,
  on the spot, a call and response—
  after all, it was the Golden Age,
still a few centuries before the signed order
  and the gate closed. So let's quaff
  the grape's blood, let's uncage the stag of love,
weave our names into our lines that sing
  of this longing to journey, against advice,
  to the mystery and the footstool,
the law and its fulfillment, the promised land.
  From the Cairo genizah we know your whereabouts,
  or most of them, because Jewish law forbids
destruction of any document with God's name.
  And everything you wrote had God's name.
  You made it to Egypt, but in Fustat
you went back to your old carousing,
  writing poems celebrating lutes and dancers,
  their ankle bracelets and their black hair:
I would fall for them all, you chanted
  at the poetry contest, *for their perilous red mouths.*
  For their silver bells of apples and pomegranates.
How could you put the world behind you
  when you were still in love with it?
  Yehuda, we journeyed to the plaza named for you
and for a few Euros ordered espressos
  and fantas and inquired of someone—anyone—
  how far the empty synagogue?
Why does this Jewish Quarter have no Jews?
  Let's have more lutes, you commanded:
  The foolish heart forgets how old it is.

Finally you sold your expensive turban,
  left Egypt in a rough boat, and sailed
  into the hands of God. You stole into
the storehouse of poetry, crept inside
  and sealed the door, turning into legend.
  Did you touch foot on that elusive soil?
Did you bow down at the Wall?
  Or did you die in your desire?
  Don't fear, Yehuda. Over the years
your poems became prayers we sing
  in the synagogue, as the Torah is lifted,
  as the congregation rises, chanted
on the day of mourning, the day
  we remember not one but two temples
  destroyed, Jerusalem laid to waste,
the people dispersed. Your love poems,
  it's true, were made of dew and fire,
  but your real instrument was your soul,
which you strummed sweetly, like a harp,
  like this warm wind breezing through these roses—
  our small portion of paradise, even in this exile.

After Reading Martin Buber

Because you were meditating
on the holy books

when the stranger knocked,
you didn't notice

his haggard face and, in your haste
to return

to studying some minor law,
you missed completely

the point of his questions
so you did not answer

those he did not ask.
And when you discovered

in the next day's news
that he killed himself,

you came to believe
that each encounter

must be presented
with one's whole being.

From Spinoza's *Book of God*

My mother took these books out
of the Park Synagogue Library
and never returned them, these books

on Halevi and Maimonides and Spinoza
and the secret Jews, she snuck them out
the way she'd wrap dinner rolls in napkins

and secure them in her large black purse.
And so I'm writing about those Jews
she'd want me to honor, though

when I was thirteen I sat and stood and sat
and stood beside her during the service,
and suddenly I turned to her and said:

I don't believe this. Did she imagine
that nearly half-a-century later, I'd struggle,
late summer morning, under a glassy sky,

with you, Benito, though I'd rather call you *Baruch*,
another non-believer, who, in your *Book of God*,
say that the more we know God the more we love Him,

and how it's all about essence, and He
doesn't live in the synagogue:
somewhere else, out there: in the earth,

somewhere else, in here: the soul.
I don't believe this, we both declared,
for which I received a sideways squint

and you got excommunicated,
though clearly we believe in something,
clearly there's a perfection somewhere—

the absolute stillness of this early afternoon,
 deepening in its mixture of shadowed light.
 God, you said, like Nature, is infinite.

There's a slight quivering of honeysuckle,
 an afternoon, perhaps, like the one
 on July 27, 1656 when you were damned

by a proclamation signed by your own people:
 In accordance with the decisions
 of the angels and the saints,

with the approval of the holy God
 and the entire congregation. A child,
 as you mastered Torah and Talmud,

you heard the auto-de-fé screaming
 through your window. So to your own mind you submitted,
 excommunicating yourself before they could excommunicate
 you.

As for me, to my mother I paraphrased Dickinson:
 "Some keep the Sabbath by going to synagogue/
 I keep it staying at home."

But she didn't command me out of her presence,
 she didn't denounce me to the congregation,
 she didn't, before God, declare:

Cursed be he during the day and cursed be he during the night.
 Instead she gave me these secret books
 and the memory of her hidden bread:

"because you never know," she'd whisper.
 "You never know when you'll be on your own."
 You preferred grinding glass, the clear, fine dust,

a bedstead, an old Turkish robe, a few pair of socks
   in need of mending: no stone, no marker,
   just your one hundred and eleven books arguing

what the prophets claimed: that to know God
   it is impossible not to love God—
   you renegade, you defector, you transgressor, you Jew.

The Scribe

The golden-winged bird who pierces an opening into the egg of the world.
—Simone Weil

1

How can we tell a body in pain? Down any avenue,
say Broadway, mid-summer, mid-day: the flashy and the quick,
the overcoated minister talking trash for a dollar, the beer can-covered

unicyclist, ring in the teenager's tongue, the spiked and the flecked,
the nail in the wrist of the accordion-playing-for-God minister, severed
brilliantly against the skyscrapers. The blades and windows

of longing, the aromatherapy palace and the $2-a-palm psychic, the lump
on the breast, the shell game on the cardboard box, the jolting and the wailing
and the dealing, birds encased in plastic, trees growing through plaster.

Not the heart's ache only, memory of the pulled-back hair, your mother's
exploding laughter, but the packed subway car, the elevator shaft. If only
the updraft of winter birds, the long snow descending. If only the ancestral

woodsmoke, the huddling. Once it was possible to walk uphill.
Once it was possible to hold the taste of the wooden spoon on your tongue.
It's the visionary on the corner waving his book. It's the man who is a torso

and a tin-cup-in-his-mouth against the doorway of the famous
cinema,
pockets of our own lives sewn on the inside of his violin case
where neither gold
nor silver accompany our departure nor precious pearls. It's the
woman

beside us mouthing words into a camera for a film they will
edit us out of,
the lovers spewing on the sidewalk, the second-story opera
singer vocalizing.
We shape ourselves into hard forms to make a career out of
death. Rest

assured: we will not be cut or scrutinized nor will the juices be
drained.
We will not be left unattended, psalms recited, white garments
sewn.
We will sift into the earth in unpolished pine with holes the
size of dust

and someone will place a small stone if only a groundskeeper
or the ordained one or the wind carrying sand from the great
city.
Woe another hour has gone. Rest assured. Someone is setting
this all down.

2

In the narrow store on Essex Street, for example, an ancient
scribe-
of-the-Book crouches before a scroll laid out like a stretched
sheet
on the splintered wooden counter, shadowed from the evening
glare.

He clutches a quill plucked from a kosher goose, its indelible
black ink
prepared from vegetables, and inscribes onto the dead flesh of
a goat
the inspired and accounted-for words and letters and if he
misspells or slips

or jerks he fasts and purifies himself in clear water and starts
again, this
chronicler of the Holy of Holies, oracular, tall and then,
bearded and established,
white ear-locks, cap pinned to white hair, peering over the
parchments

threaded like pieces of cloth for a gown or a shroud, each cell
and bone of him inflamed, his handwriting steady as if
stitching skin to skin,
his eyes staring onto the white surface as if into a door they
could open,

as if his fixed attention could trace the script into a perfection
so singular
it will be memorized and recited before the people for another
century—
the agonies and dream-visions, the propagations and
prognostications,

the secret codes and numbers and wonders and hidden
correspondences
that will puzzle and saturate, savage and perplex, ravishing,
furious,
in this city where we are forced to look every which way for our
lives.

In this city where we walk down Broadway from the celebrated
hospital,

dazed and silent and solicitous in the sidewalk explosion of
watches and smoke.
To be the color of dead leaves, like certain unnoticed insects. To
desire

nothing more than to be alone. To witness the cardinal's blood-
red flight
out of the sweetgum tree, the snow falling, alive in its mission,
into a curious
happiness, the misty distance, a small place, a dust mote in a
cow's eye.

Or to be a junco, the sunflower seed it pecks at in the frozen
earth.
Or a mottled grouse, its inconspicuous song, its thrumming
wings.
Or the golden-winged bird who pierces an opening into the egg
of the world.

G-d

Not even in representation, figure
or shape, nothing we can imagine
or create, no structure or sound or phrase—

not even symbols or color, formulas
or equations, nothing we can mold—
what we are incapable of calling out

or writing down. Our houses
are candles and stained glass,
in our pantries scrolls of words

we kiss and dance before.
The presence of beauty is without form,
and so the middle letter is erased,

spelling a word we can never pronounce,
our tongues stumbling for a vowel,
a syllable forbidden to be said,

for the sound itself is only a sign
of the original silence.
And what is it but silence after all,

the spaces we fill in with our prayers,
our actions with blessings? Here,
each of our images is graven

as we crave and carve the name
in our lower case, our imaginations
sealed in museums, wrung out in metal

and glass and stone, bound in ink
and cloth, where words follow
in their necessity out of the place

they fade into the way we shape the air
with our skins full of breath and bones
that walk, become earth, and are perfect.

The Whole Mishpocha

for Gerald Stern and Millie Terman

Clearly your Jewish soul was out hunting mine,
Stern said in his hand-scrawled yellow-lined note
I'm reading the day after he died.

Born in 1925, same year as my mother
who said: *We breathed. We were Jewish.*
You both had the Depression and the Big War

and Eisenhower's great America and houses of ticky-tacky
and lunch counters and Vietnam and that beautiful tragic
  President
and the radicals and that *meshuga* Tricky Dicky

and all that nuclear mishigas to look forward to,
both Polish-Ukrainian, both commanded by the laws
of the same wild God who never leaves us alone—

Stern in dirty Pittsburgh, Millie in dirty Cleveland,
both poets—Stern a macher, a real landsman,
Millie a bissel shtick with rhyme at bar mitzvahs, weddings,

Stern with a little more Yiddishe Kop
and Millie a whole mishmosh of heimish,
both nudging me not to be a putz, but a mensch,

at which I failed, my soul on the loose for atonement,
wondering why I haven't written a poem about Jeremiah,
who every Thursday at 2:30 visits our Prophets class where

in our cracked voices we kvetch aloud the bad news to the
  Philistines,
the Moabites, the Ammonites, warning that *every head is bald*
and every beard is shorn, and the Edomites, progeny of Esau,

whose renouncing of his birthright marked him and his
descendants,
and when I open my heart to the plea of the needy, and judge
not
the case of an orphan, I can drink the fruit of the vine with
Gerry,

and especially Millie who, New Year's Eve in Jerusalem,
drunk on Manishevitz in the King David Hotel, hoisted herself
up
onto the bed and lifted her full glass in a l' Chayim not to
Jeremiah,

that bullfrog, but her whole mishpocha, in that holy city, finally.

Notes

p. 21 "Abraham Breaking the Idols": From a midrash told in Genesis Rabbah 38.13 and in the Quran 21:51-9

p. 23 "Eloquence": Moses' deciding between the coins and the coal: Midrash Shemot Rabbah 1.31

p. 26"All Vows": a translation of Kol Nidre, the service that precedes the Yom Kippur service.

p. 27 "Avodah": "Work, worship, service." The prayers in the Yom Kippur service describing the moments when, in Temple times, the high priest takes on the sins of the congregation.

p. 35 "My Grandfather in Green": The sentence *He came, sat down, and at once fell asleep,* appears in Chagall's autobiography, *My Life, translated by Elisabeth Abbot (De Capo Press, 1994)*

p. 42 "L'Dor va' dor": from generation to generation

p. 51 "Crazy Meshugenahs": "God looked into the Torah and created the world. Man looks into Torah and sustains the world."—Midrash Rabah

p. 65 "Singer Among the Pigeons": Gimpel—from Isaac Singer's famous tale "Gimpel the Fool."

p. 78 "Her Conversion": "...as in a field of barley"—from "The Book of Ruth."

p. 84 "The Sofer": Jewish scribe trained to write Torah scrolls

p. 85 "Hasidim in New Square, New York Hear Carp Speaking Hebrew": A true story! https://www.nytimes.com/2003/03/15/nyregion/miracle-dream-prank-fish-talks-town-buzzes.html

p. 93 "Ruth Bader Ginsberg": The final quote is found in Proverbs 31:16

p. 98 "The Last Mikvah": The poem describes the tahara, the cleansing of the body, part of the Chevra Kadisha, (holy society) that prepares the boy for burial.

p. 106 "It's All Possible": Riad Saleh Hussein: (1952-1982) Syrian poet from the Aleppo province. He was mute and deaf, yet published four collections of poetry. His poetry revolutionized open verse poetry in Arabic and he is much admired today. A collection of his poetry was translated into English by Saleh Razzouk and Philip Terman: *Tango Under a Narrow Roof* (Bitter Oleander Press, 2021).

p. 108 Mahmoud Darwish, Palestinian poet (1941-2008); Yehuda Amichai, Israeli poet (1924-2000).

p. 109 "Yehuda Halevi's Journey to the Holy Land": A geniza is a room where sacred Hebrew manuscripts (especially those that mention God's name) are kept.

p. 117 "The Scribe": Simone Weil quote from *Waiting for God* (Harper and Row, 1973), translated by Emma Crauford.

p. 121 "The Whole Mishpocha": Gerald Stern, beloved American poet, 1925-2022

Acknowledgments

Grateful acknowledgment to the following journals and anthologies where the following poems originally appeared:

The Blue Lyra Review: "Teaching My Daughters the Mourner's Kaddish"
Chautauqua Literary Review: "Hasidim in New Square, New York Hear Carp Speaking Hebrew"
The Connecticut Review: "The Dress Factory"
Connotation Press: "Abraham's Breaking of the Idols"
The Forward: "The Fates"
The Fourth River: "The Last Torah Reader"
Image: "My Grandfather in Green"
Jewish Book Council: "Writing Jewish"
Jewish Currents: "Tormented Meshugenahs"
Jewish Journal: "Again, These Blintzes"
"The house without a clock..."
Joyful Noise: An Anthology Of Spiritual Literature: "G-d"
The Kafka Project: "Kaddish for Kafka"
The Kenyon Review: "A Cast of Thousands"
The Laurel Review: "The Bris"
The Mid-American Review: "What We Own"
Minyan: "God's Speech"
North Appalachian Review: "Jewing Him Down"
One Magazine (Jacar Press): "It's All Possible"
One Art: "Kol Nidre"

The New England Review: "The Schwitz"
New Voices: Contemporary Writers Confronting the Holocaust: "Night of the Broken Glass"
99 Poems for the 99 Percent: "Albert Einstein at the Soup Kitchen"
101 Poems for the Third Millennium: "Isaiah at Rest"
The Pittsburgh Post-Gazette: "A Minyan Plus One"
Poetica: "The Everlasting Light"
Poetry: "Eloquence," "The Russian Jewish Woman Poet Termanovsky," "The House of Sages," "My Father's Scale" (as "Attachments"), "G-d"
Tiferet Journal: "Our Scriptures"
Tikkun: "The Synagogue in Oil City," "Drying the Torah"
Vox Populi: "A Minyan Plus One," "Darwin and Amichai Share Poems in Heaven"
West Branch: "Isaiah at Rest"
Zeek: "At the Wailing Wall," "Shalom Is My Middle Name," "Her Voice" (as "The Exile"), "Spinoza's Book of God" "Halevi's Journey to the Holy Land," "From Moses to Moses"
"A Minyan Plus One" was translated into Hebrew by Hagit Grossman and appeared in the Israeli journal, *Iton 77*

Much gratitude for your wisdom, healing and rachmonis:

— Larry Berg, JoAnn Dempler, Tom Doerr, Brian Engle, Fred Evans, Marty Forchheimer, Cantor Michal Grey-Shaffer, The Hoods, Lori Jakiela, Seth Labovitz, Al Maginnes, Ann Pancake, Jane McCafferty, Barb McCloskey, Marty and Julie Meyer, John Miller, Scott Minar, Baruch November, Ann Pancake, Tom Peters, Jeff Powell, Saleh Razzouk, Dan Roche, Judy Rock, Mike Simms, Rick St. John, James and Lynn Stewart, David Swerdlow, David Terman, Stuart Terman, Susan Terman, Tony Vallone, Ben Vincent, Kevan Yenerall.

Special thanks: Rodger Kamenetz: for the inspiration of his writings; Julia Knobloch: stellar editor, for her patience and insight; Yehoshua November for his spiritual guidance and friendship; Jaqueline Osherow, whose poetry has been a model; Larry Yudelson: for including me in his commitment to Jewish poetry.

Thanks to the artist Bill Farran for permission to use his block print, "The Synagogue at Yarmolyntsi, Ukraine," from his book *Lost Treasures: The Wooden Synagogues of Eastern Europe* (Independently published, 2023) www.billfarran.com or lostreasures@yahoo.com

About the Author

Philip Terman's most recent books of poetry are *My Blossoming Everything* (Saddle Road Press, 2024), *This Crazy Devotion* (Broadstone, 2020), *Our Portion: New and Selected Poems* (Autumn House, 2015) and, as co-translator, *Tango Beneath a Narrow Ceiling: The Selected poems of Riad Saleh Hussein* (Bitter Oleander, 2021). His poems and essays have appeared in journals, including *Poetry Magazine, The Kenyon Review, Tikkun, The Georgia Review* and *Poetry International,* and anthologies, including *The Bloomsbury Anthology of Contemporary Poetry, 101 Poets for the Next Millennium, Blood to Remember: American Poets on the Holocaust,* and *Joyful Noise: An Anthology of Spiritual Literature, Extraordinary Rendition: American Writers on Palestine.* Retired from Clarion University, he served as co-director of the Chautauqua Writers Festival for 14 years. Currently, he directs The Bridge Literary Arts Center in Venango County, PA and is co-curator the Jewish Poetry Reading Series, sponsored by the Jewish Community Center of Buffalo. Recipient of the Anna Davidson Rosenberg Award for Poems on the Jewish Experience, Terman conducts poetry workshops and coaches writing hither and yon. He has collaborated with composers, visual artists, and performs his poetry with the jazz band Catro.
https://philipterman.my.canva.site

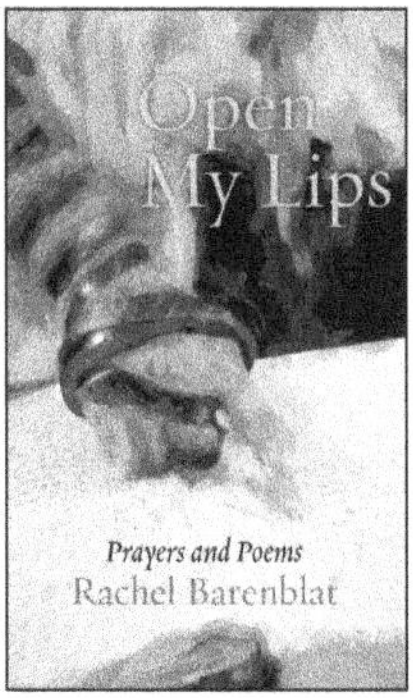

Open My Lips: Prayers and Poems by Rachel Barenblat

"Barenblat's God is a personal God—one who lets her cry on His shoulder, and who rocks her like a colicky baby. These poems bridge the gap between the ineffable and the human. This collection will bring comfort to those with a religion of their own, as well as those seeking a relationship with some kind of higher power."
—Satya Robyn, author of *The Most Beautiful Thing*

Words for Blessing the World: Poems in Hebrew and English by Herbert J. Levine

"These writings express a profoundly earth-based theology in a language that is clear and comprehensible. These are works to study and learn from."
—Rodger Kamenetz, author of *The Jew in the Lotus*

Shiva Moon: Poems by Maxine Silverman

"The poems, deeply felt, are spare, spoken in a quiet but compelling voice, as if we were listening in to her inner life. This book is a precious record of the transformation saying Kaddish can bring."
—Howard Schwartz, author of *The Library of Dreams*

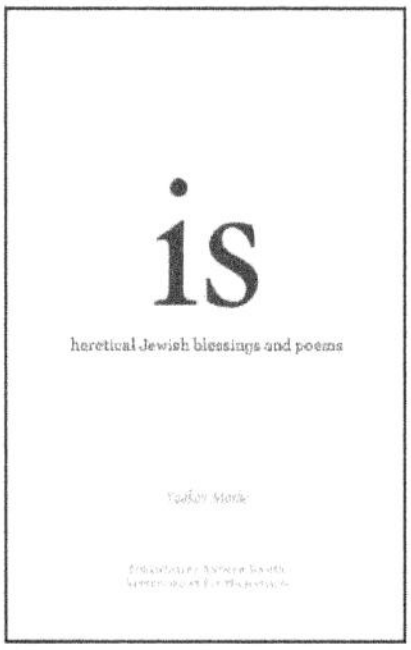

is: heretical Jewish blessings and poems by Yaakov Moshe (Jay Michaelson)

"Finally, Torah that speaks to and through the lives we are actually living: expanding the tent of holiness to embrace what has been cast out, elevating what has been kept down, advancing what has been held back, reveling in questions, revealing contradictions."
—Eden Pearlstein, aka eprhyme

Texts to the Holy: Poems
by Rachel Barenblat

"These poems are remarkable, radiating a love of God that is full bodied, innocent, raw, pulsating, hot, drunk. I can hardly fathom their faith but am grateful for the vistas they open. I will sit with them, and invite you to do the same."
—Merle Feld, author of *A Spiritual Life*

The Sabbath Bee: Love Songs to Shabbat
by Wilhelmina Gottschalk

"Torah, say our sages, has seventy faces. As these prose poems reveal, so too does Shabbat. Here we meet Shabbat as familiar housemate, as the child whose presence transforms a family, as a spreading tree, as an annoying friend who insists on being celebrated, as a woman, as a man, as a bee, as the ocean."
—Rachel Barenblat, author of *The Velveteen Rabbi's Haggadah*

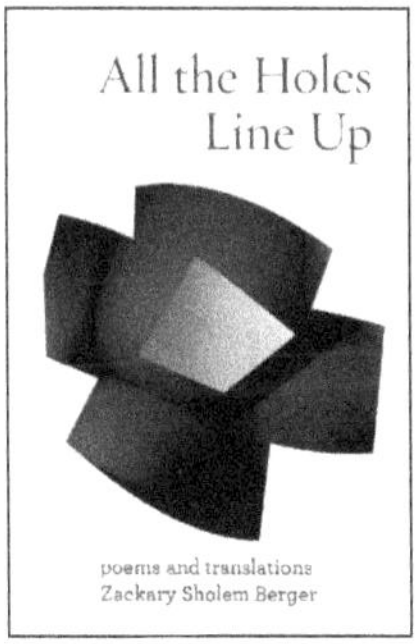

All the Holes Line Up: Poems and Translations
by Zackary Sholem Berger

"Spare and precise, Berger's poems gaze unflinchingly at—but also celebrate—human imperfection in its many forms. And what a delight that Berger also includes in this collection a handful of his resonant translations of some of the great Yiddish poets." —Yehoshua November, author of *God's Optimism* and *Two World Exist*

How to Bless the New Moon: Songs of the Sovereign and the Icon
by Rachel Kann

"Rachel Kann is a master wordsmith. Her poems are rich in content, packed with life's wisdom and imbued with soul. May this collection of her work enable more of the world to enjoy her offerings."
—Sarah Yehudit Schneider, author of *You Are What You Hate* and *Kabbalistic Writings on the Nature of Masculine and Feminine*

Into My Garden
by David Caplan

"The beauty of Caplan's book is that it is not polemical. It does not set out to win an argument or ask you whether you've put your tefillin on today. These gentle poems invite the reader into one person's profound, ambiguous religious experience."
—*The Jewish Review of Books*

Between the Mountain and the Land is the Lesson: Poetic Midrash on Sacred Community
by Abe Mezrich

"Abe Mezrich cuts straight back to the roots of the Midrashic tradition, sermonizing as a poet, rather than idealogue. Best of all, Abe knows how to ask questions and avoid the obvious answers."
—Jake Marmer, author of *Jazz Talmud*

NOKADDISH: Poems in the Void
by Hanoch Guy Kaner

"A subversive, midrashic play with meanings–specifically Jewish meanings, and then the reversal and negation of these meanings."
—Robert G. Margolis

An Added Soul: Poems for a New Old Religion
by Herbert J. Levine

"These poems are remarkable, radiating a love of God that is full bodied, innocent, raw, pulsating, hot, drunk. I can hardly fathom their faith but am grateful for the vistas they open. I will sit with them, and invite you to do the same."
—Merle Feld, author of *A Spiritual Life*.

What Remains
by David Curzon

"Aphoristic, ekphrastic, and precise revelations animate WHAT REMAINS. In his stunning rewriting of Psalm 1 and other biblical passages, Curzon shows himself to be a fabricator, a collector, and an heir to the literature, arts, and wisdom traditions of the planet."
—Alicia Ostriker, author of *The Volcano and After*

The Shortest Skirt in Shul
by Sass Oron

"These poems exuberantly explore gender, Torah, the masks we wear, and the way our bodies (and the ways we wear them) at once threaten stable narratives, and offer the kind of liberation that saves our lives."
—Alicia Jo Rabins, author of *Divinity School*, composer of *Girls In Trouble*

Walking Triptychs
by Ilya Gutner

These are poems from when I walked about Shanghai and thought about the meaning of the Holocaust.

Book of Failed Salvation
by Julia Knobloch

"These beautiful poems express a tender longing for spiritual, physical, and emotional connection. They detail a life in movement—across distances, faith, love, and doubt."
—David Caplan, author of *Into My Garden*

Daily Blessings: Poems on Tractate Berakhot by Hillel Broder

"Hillel Broder does not just write poetry about the Talmud; he also draws out the Talmud's poetry, finding lyricism amidst legality and re-setting the Talmud's rich images like precious gems in end-stopped lines of verse."
—Ilana Kurshan, author of *If All the Seas Were Ink*

The Missing Jew: Poems 1976-2022 by Rodger Kamenetz

"How does Rodger Kamenetz manage to have so singular a voice and at the same time precisely encapsulate the world view of an entire generation (also mine) of text-hungry American Jews born in the middle of the twentieth century?"
—Jacqueline Osherow, author of *Ultimatum from Paradise* and *My Lookalike at the Krishna Temple: Poems*

The Red Door: A dark fairy tale told in poems by Shawn C. Harris

"The Red Door, like its poet author Shawn C. Harris, transcends genres and identities. It is an exploration in crossing worlds. It brings together poetry and story telling, imagery and life events, spirit and body, the real and the fantastic, Jewish past and Jewish present, to spin one tale."
—Einat Wilf, author of *The War of Return*

The Matter of Families by Robert H. Deluty

"Robert Deluty's career-spanning collection of New and Selected poems captures the essence of his work: the power of love, joy, and connection, all tied together with the poet's glorious sense of humor. This book is Deluty's masterpiece."
—Richard M. Berlin, M.D., author of *Freud on My Couch*

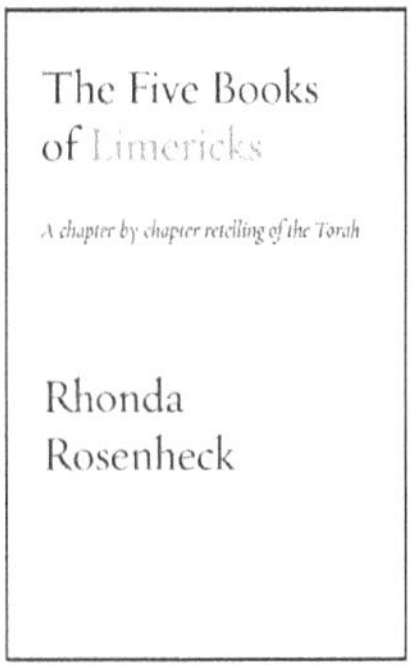

The Five Books of Limericks
by Rhonda Rosenheck

"A biblical commentary that is truly unique. Each chapter of the Torah is distilled into its own limerick, leading the reader to reconsider the meaning of the original text, and opening avenues for interpretation that are both fun and insightful."
—Rabbi Hillel Norry

Bits and Pieces
by Edward Pomerantz

"A stunning tapestry of family life in the 40s and 50s. Like all great poetry, Pomerantz's work expands after reading. Each poem is exquisitely structured, often with a stunning ending, into a masterful whole."
—Alan Ziegler, editor of *SHORT: An International Anthology*

Words for a Dazzling Firmament: Poems/ Readings on Bereishit Through Shemot
by Abe Mezrich

"Mezrich is a cultivated craftsman— interpretively astute, sonically deliberate, and spiritually cunning."
—Zohar Atkins, author of *Nineveh*

Everything Thaws
by R. B. Lemberg

"Full of glacier-sharp truths, and moments revealed between words like bodies beneath melting permafrost. As it becomes increasingly plain how deeply our world is shaped by war and climate change and grief and anger, articulating that shape feels urgent and necessary and painful and healing."
—Ruthanna Emrys, author of *A Half-Built Garden*

Ode to the Dove
An illustrated, bilingual edition of a Yiddish poem by Abraham Sutzkever
Zackary Sholem Berger, translator
Liora Ostroff, Illustrator

"An elegant volume for lovers of poetry."
—Justin Cammy, translator of *Sutzkever, From the Vilna Ghetto to Nuremberg: Memoir and Testimony*

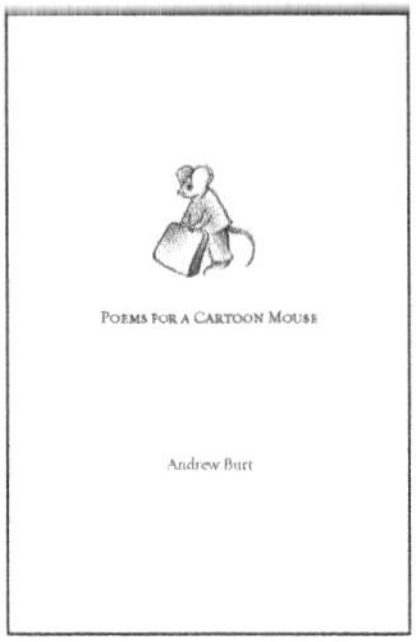

Poems for a Cartoon Mouse
by Andrew Burt

"Andrew Burt's poetry magnifies the vanishingly small line between danger and safety. This collection asks whether order is an illusion that veils chaos, or vice-versa, juxtaposing images from the Bible with animated films."
—Ari Shapiro, host of NPR's *All Things Considered*

Old Shul
by Pinny Bulman

"Nostalgia gives way to a tender theology, a softly chuckling illumination from within the heart of/as a beautiful, broken sanctuary, somehow both gritty and fragile, grimy and iridescent – not unlike faith itself."
—Jake Marmer, author of *Cosmic Diaspora*

Feet In L.A., But My Womb Lives In Jerusalem, My Breath In Vermont
by Lori Levy

"Reading through Lori Levy's new book of poems takes my breath away. With no pretense whatsoever, they leap, alive, from the page until this reader felt as if she were living Levy's life. How does the author do it?"
—Mary Jo Balistreri, author of *Still*

Printed in the USA
CPSIA information can be obtained
at www.ICGtesting.com
CBHW022113300724
12440CB00009B/133

9 781963 475319